EMILY PFEIFFER

Emily Pfeiffer (1827–1890) was a prolific and well-respected poet and essayist, whose work has only recently started to receive the academic attention and literary recognition it merits. A courageous and outspoken feminist, Pfeiffer used her considerable literary influence to expose and exploit sensitive gender issues of her day. During the years between 1873 and 1884 – years that witnessed the unprecedented growth of the women's movement – Pfeiffer was forced to confront the growing mismatch between the two key ideologies that framed her life: Christianity and feminism. The result of this conflict was the publication of a series of works which show Pfeiffer to be a highly original avant-garde poet. In this study, Prudence Brand reads the complex, transgressive force of these works and identifies Pfeiffer as a spiritual emancipationist dedicated to establishing a place for women within both the Christian community and society at large.

Prudence Brand was formally trained in medical and scientific subjects, and worked for many years as a secondary Science teacher. She has spent the last fifteen years developing her interest in Victorian feminist poetry, and was awarded her PhD from Royal Holloway, University of London, in 2012.

Emily Pfeiffer, *Under the Aspens, Lyrical and Dramatic*
(London: Kegan Paul, 1882)
Reproduced by kind permission of the Syndics of Cambridge University Library

EMILY PFEIFFER

Poet, Feminist, Iconoclast

Prudence Brand

COUNTRY SETTING

EMILY PFEIFFER
Poet, Feminist, Iconoclast

This edition typeset and produced by Country Setting
Kingsdown, Kent, CT14 8ES UK

www.countrysetting.co.uk

Printed and bound in Great Britain

Frontispiece etching of Emily Pfeiffer
by Leopold Lowenstam reproduced by kind permission
of the Syndics of Cambridge University Library

Cover design by Anna Trussler

A catalogue record for this book is available
from the British Library

ISBN: PB: 978-0-9559998-5-7

for
ADAM

Contents

Acknowledgements   ix

Emily Jane Pfeiffer: A Biographical Overview   1

Introduction   9

1   Writing Against the Bias   19
2   Changing Christian Images   53
3   Integrating Mythologies   83
4   Re-Authorising the Scriptures   105

Conclusion   145

Bibliography   149

Index   165

Acknowledgements

Many of the ideas for this book come from my doctoral thesis on 'Emily Pfeiffer and Victorian Women's Religious Poetry' (Royal Holloway University of London, 2012). This thesis, in turn, grew out of my MA dissertation entitled 'Upsetting Women: A Poet and her Heroine in *The Rhyme of the Lady of the Rock* by Emily Pfeiffer' (Open University, 2004). I would therefore like to thank Joanna Gondris and Naomi Lightman (2004), and Vicky Greenaway and my supervisor, Anne Varty (2012), for their important contributions towards the development of this book. In addition, I owe a great debt of gratitude to Nick de Somogyi for reading the manuscript and for his much-appreciated expertise. My thanks also go to Simon and Anna Trussler at Country Setting for transforming my manuscript into print. My thanks go too to the Syndics of Cambridge University Library for granting me permission to reproduce the image of Emily Pfeiffer. I would also like to thank Richard Suggett, Brian Malaws, Hilary Malaws, and Ann Kinsler for their input. To the staff and librarians of Aberystwyth University Library, the British Library, the London Library, Newtown Library, and the Royal Holloway University Library, I also extend my thanks.

My love and thanks go to my husband, Adam, for his constant interest in my work and for his unfailing enthusiasm and encouragement; and to my much-loved children, Nicholas and Emily, for their support.

Prudence Brand
Twickenham, March 2015

Emily Jane Pfeiffer
A Biographical Overview

EMILY JANE PFEIFFER (1827–1890) was born at the home of her maternal grandparents at Milford, just outside Newtown, Montgomeryshire.[1] Her father, Thomas Richard Davis, was an Oxfordshire army officer who lost his estate when his bank collapsed. Her mother, Emily Tilsley, was the daughter of a family of landowners in the Parish of Aberhafesp, Montgomeryshire.[2] Growing up in a house overlooking the River Severn, the young Emily Jane Davis was exposed to influences that were to add a Celtic flavour to much of her poetry.

The population of Newtown, the major centre of handloom weaving in mid-Wales, quadrupled in the forty years between 1801 and 1841. Technological innovation, in the form of the carding engine and spinning jenny, changed the flannel industry irrevocably, and consequently Newtown became a hub of discontent as machines took the place of employees and mills had to be closed. The Tilsley family was not immune to the wider effects of these changes as it is recorded that in 1831 one of Davis's relations, a banker, was forced to sell his mills to pay his creditors.[3] Growing up so close to Newtown, Davis would have seen mill-girls and factory workers working for miserable wages; she would have heard of the formation of the British Women's Movement, then in its embryonic stages; she would have known about the Rebecca Riots that broke out in pockets of rural Wales in 1839, and the Chartist movement that was starting to gain momentum in South Wales. All these, set against the rapid construction of Nonconformist chapels in Wales, would have made an indelible impression on the young Emily Davis.

During her childhood Emily and her sisters were taught by their father who, in the 1851 Census, described himself as an artist. When Emily was fifteen, he funded the publication of her first literary work, *The Holly-Branch: an Album for 1843*.[4] This publication showcases her literary, musical, and artistic precocity but, without financial backing, the future looked bleak for her as she entered maturity.[5] Fortunately a friend invited her to join her on holiday in Europe, and subsequently Davis spent time in London where she met her future husband, Jürgen Edward Pfeiffer, a German merchant from Holstein.[6] After their marriage in 1850, Pfeiffer, fourteen years her senior, was able to provide her with the money she needed to further her education. T. D. Olverson, writing about Emily Pfeiffer's 'Political Hellenism', notes that she was a 'keen student of Greek, philosophy, sculpture, architecture and drama' (subjects that informed her sonnets 'Hellas' and 'Studies from the Antique'), receiving 'intellectual encouragement' from Professor John Stuart Blackie and Mark Pattison, Rector of Lincoln College.[7] In London, Edward Pfeiffer and his wife took up residence in a villa situated halfway between Clapham Common and Wandsworth Road.[8]

In 1856, the artist and activist Barbara Leigh Smith [Bodichon] (1827–91) and Bessie Rayner Parkes [Belloc] (1829–1925) launched the *Englishwoman's Journal*, published by Emily Faithful, the founder of the Victoria Press in 1860. The 'ladies of Langham Place' supported women's rights and backed Caroline Norton's campaign for reform of the marriage and divorce laws. In 1865, the group organised petitions for the Woman's Suffrage Bill to be presented to Parliament by John Stuart Mill (1806–73). In 1869, Mill (supported by Harriet Taylor before her death in 1858) published his book *The Subjection of Women*, promoting gender equality in education, employment, marriage, law, and suffrage.[9] Yet right from the start of her literary career, Emily Pfeiffer had railed against the inhumane divorce laws that separated mothers and children, her later poem 'Outlawed: A Rhyme for the Time' (1884) likening the politicians who passed these draconian laws to slave owners. Throughout her adult life she bent her exceptional literary talents to the task of promoting women's emancipation and, in 1885, *Contemporary Review* published in full her eighteen-page article entitled 'The Suffrage for Women' in which she referred to an 'unseen hand' lifting mankind from the brute to a higher plane of spiritual existence.

In 1857, at the age of thirty, Pfeiffer published a prose work entitled *Valisneria, or A Midsummer Day's Dream*. This was followed by her blank-verse novel, *Margaret; or, The Motherless* (1861), a publication which reflects the influence of *Aurora Leigh*, the famous blank-verse novel published by Elizabeth Barrett Browning in 1856.[10] In April 1871, a brief correspondence between Pfeiffer and Charles Darwin saw her grappling with the theory of evolution and the concept of natural selection.[11] In the years between 1873 and her death in 1890, Emily Pfeiffer published eight volumes of poetry, two travel books (one of them a mixed-genre work), an emancipationist volume called *Women and Work* (1888), and a large number of articles and poems printed mainly by the *Spectator* and *Contemporary Review*. Increasingly recognised in intellectual circles as a poet of high standing, Pfeiffer was one of a growing number of women to challenge the social, political, and legal conditions that kept women subject to patriarchal domination. Olverson writes that after the Pfeiffers moved into their new house on West Hill in Putney,[12] they threw parties attended by the 'influential scholars, commentators and political figures of the day'.[13] Alluding to Pfeiffer's interest in Ancient Greece, Olverson records that 'upwards of fifty ladies apparently responded to the call [to come in ancient Greek dress], including the feminist writer Frances Power Cobbe and the Greek scholar Anna Swanwick'.[14] Now Pfeiffer was able to enjoy her success – a success marred, however, by a small number of sexist reviews.

In 1873 Pfeiffer's first volume of poems, *Gerard's Monument, and Other Poems*, received so much praise that a second edition followed in 1878, boasting ten complimentary 'Notes' from the earlier edition. Typical of these is the review from the *Daily Telegraph*:

> It is refreshing to come on a volume of pure and simple poetry, such as [*Gerard's Monument*] by Emily Pfeiffer, which has undoubted claims to high praise in these 'degenerate days' of poetic inspiration. Mrs. Pfeiffer is really a poetess . . . The volume is full of beauty; one sure to be delightedly perused by those who can appreciate true poetic feeling and genuine unrestrained expression.[15]

This 'metrical romance' was nevertheless attacked by an anonymous reviewer writing for *The Times*, who criticised not only her verse but also her right, as a woman, to write it. Patronisingly conceding that the piece is 'full of fancy and feeling', he goes on:

> When Shakespeare, or Milton, or Byron, or Wordsworth writes, this conflict seems as much in the order of nature as a storm at sea, whereas female poetry . . . is too apt to give us the idea of a desperate attempt to stir a storm in a teacup . . . Whatever is said, the fact remains that the female mind has seldom or never produced poetry of the first order . . . [Women] have tried and they have failed – because it was not in them.[16]

Pfeiffer retaliated strongly against the article. '[As] a woman,' she wrote,

> I cannot but lift up a protesting voice against any attempt to close 'our case', while every day is bringing fresh witnesses into the action . . . That we can be speculated about now in this advanced stage of the world's history more as if we were some extinct species than beings who have stood side by side with man from the beginning, is in itself a striking result of that tyranny of circumstances which has retarded female development.[17]

In 1876 Pfeiffer published another collection of poems in a volume aptly entitled *Poems*, and here again she received many excellent reviews. A year later, in 1877, Pfeiffer's publisher, Kegan Paul & Co., published a lavish promotion of her poetry in the *Spectator*. Included in this promotion were glowing reviews exemplified by the following citations. From the *Daily Telegraph*: 'Mrs. Pfeiffer's 'Poems' are worthy of the name'; from the *Westminster Review*: 'In her sonnets . . . she puts forth her strength'; and from the *Spectator* itself: 'The verse is melodious and flowing'.[18] And yet, in contrast to these and other excellent reviews published by the *Spectator*, a critic writing for the *Pall Mall Gazette* – either because he opposed women's emancipation or because he lacked the intellectual capacity to grasp the subtlety of Pfeiffer's verse – wrote a review that was both insulting and biased. This review is discussed below.

Although redolent of the poetics of the Romantic period, Pfeiffer's lyric poems 'The Crown of Song', 'Hymn to the Dark Christmas of 1874', and her sonnets 'The Chrysalis' and 'The Coming Day', discussed below, are complex poems with enduringly challenging religious subtexts. Widely respected as a formidable sonneteer, Pfeiffer's sonnets were described by the reviewer for the *Spectator* as 'among the finest in the language'.[19]

Pfeiffer's Welsh blank-verse novel *Glân-Alarch, His Silence and Song* (1877) was swiftly followed by *Quarterman's Grace and Other Poems* (1879). 'Madonna Dūnya', the longest poem in the *Quarterman's Grace* collection, had previously been published in its entirety in *Contemporary Review* (1877–8).[20] Then came *Sonnets and Songs* (1880) and *Under the Aspens, Lyrical and Dramatic* (1882). In that same year, a fire at the warehouse of her publishers, Messrs. Kegan Paul, Trench & Co., destroyed the stereotype 'plates' preserving the typeset texts of *Gerard's Monument, Glân-Alarch, His Silence and Song, Poems,* and *Sonnets and Songs,* although the plates of *Under the Aspens* seem to have survived the fire. After this calamity Pfeiffer was taken ill; nevertheless, between 1882 and 1885 she toured Scotland, Turkey, Greece, and North America, and published two major works: *The Rhyme of the Lady of the Rock, and How It Grew* (1884), discussed below, and her travelogue-style work, *Flying Leaves from East and West* (1885). A year later Pfeiffer re-published some of her best-loved sonnets from *Sonnets and Songs* with a collection of new ones in a volume entitled *Sonnets* (1886).

In 1883, on her tour of Greece, Pfeiffer was shocked to find the Parthenon a 'pathetic ruin'. She also protested against the fifth book of Plato's *Republic*, writing angrily:

> Was ever an outrage so callous perpetrated on the human affections as that advocated in this book of the divine Plato . . . ? I turn from the wisdom of Greece; it has become to me foolishness. I turn from the Acropolis, where stands the golden Parthenon . . . I seek a wisdom higher and more fruitful than the unmated Reason . . . I aspire to equal justice, I look for unbounded liberty . . . Here, then, for the first time the mighty bronze image of the Zeus-born Athene . . . was confronted with the herald of Jesus of Nazareth, a name around which the love and faith of unlettered disciples had already woven the pregnant myth, if no more than myth it be, which was to supplant that other.[21]

Even the briefest perusal of *Flying Leaves from East and West* renders it transparent that an important motive behind Pfeiffer's descriptions of her visit to a harem in Smyrna, and of her visit to a Mormon community in Salt Lake City, was to draw the attention of her readership to man's inhumanity to woman. Drawing parallels between the slavery of women in the harems of the East and the illegal 'stone of offence' against wives in polygamous marriages in the West, Pfeiffer tenaciously promulgated her emancipationist cause.

As the nineteenth century moved towards its final decade, Pfeiffer became associated with a London coterie consisting of what Ana Parejo Vadillo describes as 'well-established poets, writers, novelists and dramatists'.[22] A late-Victorian poet, Pfeiffer rubbed shoulders with poets such as Katharine Tynan Hinkson (whose poems, like Pfeiffer's, were regularly printed in the *Spectator*), and poets of the *fin-de-siècle* such as A. Mary F. Robinson, Mathilde Blind, Rosamund Marriott Watson (Tomson), Louisa Bevington, Michael Field, and Augusta Webster. The poet Emily Hickey, an ardent supporter of Irish Home Rule and Roman Catholic convert, was an especially close friend of Pfeiffer.

By now, though, Edward was becoming very frail; her life-long companion and loving support through good times and bad, he died in 1889, leaving Emily to mourn alone. Her final volume of poetry, *Flowers of the Night*, was published that year.

Almost exactly a year later, on 3 January 1890, Emily Pfeiffer herself died at Mayfield. She left property valued at over £63,000, the bulk of which was divided between three institutions involved in higher education for women: the University of Wales, Cardiff; Newnham College, Cambridge (where the Pfeiffer arch and gate, completed in 1893, can still be seen today); and Hughes Hall, the oldest postgraduate college in Cambridge (founded in 1885). The first Principal of Hughes Hall, Miss Elizabeth Hughes (1851–1925), championed the cause of co-education and freedom of worship. A Welsh scholar (with the bardic name 'Merch Myrddin'), Hughes taught at Cheltenham Ladies College and was the only woman on the committee that drafted the charter of the University of Wales where, in 1920, she received an honorary degree.

Notes

1. The 1851 Census gives Pfeiffer's birthplace as Oxford (HO 107/1578), that of her Welsh mother as Middlesex, and of her sister Caroline as Gloucestershire (HO 107/1728). Most scholars are agreed, however, that Pfeiffer was born at Milford Hall, Montgomeryshire.

2. *Collections Historical and Archaeological relating to Montgomeryshire and its Borders* 46 (1940), 114. Regarding the Tilsleys of Llwydgoed in the Parish of Aberhafesp, it states: 'The Tilsleys were connected with the banking firm of Blayney & Tilsley in Newtown.'

A BIOGRAPHICAL OVERVIEW

3. *Collections Historical*, op. cit., p. 64: 'William Tilsley of Aberhafesp built several mills renting them out to flannel manufacturers and became partner in the bank of William Pugh, Colley & Company. When it failed in 1831, he had to sell his mills to pay his creditors.'

4. Emily Davis, *The Holly-Branch, An Album for 1843* (London: John Ollivier, 1843).

5. T. D. Olverson, 'Worlds without Women: Emily Pfeiffer's Political Hellenism', *Women Writers and the Dark Side of Late-Victorian Hellenism* (London: Palgrave Macmillan, 2010), 91–100 (p. 84). Citing an unpublished article by Basil Herbertson, Olverson writes that the adult Emily Pfeiffer exhibited paintings at the Royal Academy.

6. Ibid.: 'The trip up the Rhine valley greatly expanded Emily's experience of the world and soon afterwards she spent a season in London where she met her husband and travel companion-to-be, Jürgen Edward Pfeiffer.'

7. Ibid.

8. The 1851 Census (HO 107/1578) shows Emily and Edward Pfeiffer living at 1, North Street, Wandsworth, London, with two live-in servants.

9. John Stuart Mill, *The Subjection of Women* [1869], ed. Alan Ryan (London: Penguin, 2006).

10. *Poetical Works of Elizabeth Barrett Browning* (London: Henry Frowde, 1904), pp. 374–539.

11. Emily Pfeiffer, (Letters 7411 and 7719f, vol. 19), *Correspondence of Charles Darwin* (Darwin Correspondence Project, University of Cambridge, 2007).

12. See the 1871 Census (RG 10/703). Their house, Mayfield, no longer exists but there is a block of flats called 'Mayfields' on the site.

13. Olverson, 'Worlds without Women', op. cit., pp. 84–5, citing a 'Letter held as part of the Gladstone Correspondence, British Library, authored by J. Edward Pfeiffer and dated 25 March, 1878'.

14. Ibid.

15. *Daily Telegraph*, 'Notices of the Press', first printed in *Gerard's Monument and Other Poems* (London: C. Kegan Paul, 1873) and later reprinted in the 1878 edition ('Notices', pp. 1–2).

16. 'Female Poets', *The Times*, 8 January 1874.

17. Emily Pfeiffer's letter to *The Times*, quoted in *Nineteenth-Century Women Poets*, ed. Isobel Armstrong, Joseph Bristow, and Cath Sharrock (Oxford: Clarendon, 1996), pp. 494–5.

18. Emily Pfeiffer, 'Notices of the Press' provided by C. Kegan Paul & Co., *Spectator*, 2581 (1877), p. 1597.

19. Ibid.

20. Emily Pfeiffer, 'Madonna Dūnya', *Contemporary Review* 31 (1877–8), 597–627.

21. Compare *The Republic of Plato*, trans. F. M. Cornford (Oxford: Clarendon Press, 1955): 'Which do we think right for watch-dogs: should the females guard the flock and hunt with the males . . . or should they be kept within doors as fit for no more than bearing and feeding their puppies?' (p. 145).

22. Ana Parejo Vadillo, 'Immaterial Poetics: A. Mary F. Robinson and the *Fin-de-Siècle* Poem', in *The Fin-de-Siècle Poem, English Literary Culture and the 1890s*, ed. Joseph Bristow (Athens, Ohio: Ohio University Press, 2005), p. 240.

7

Introduction

Whoever aspires to wings must be free, free of the air, free
of the sun . . . I had written of what, as a woman, I could feel
as possibly no man could; if there was toll to pay in taking
that path, I would pay it, bringing this small sacrifice to the
cause of freedom . . .

— The Poet, in Emily Pfeiffer,
The Rhyme of the Lady of the Rock, and How it Grew
(1884)

To DESCRIBE EMILY PFEIFFER both as a maker and breaker of
images seems paradoxical, yet in some ways she was just that
– an iconoplast and an iconoclast. In fact, she was quite capable of
making and breaking images in a single poetic work. Regardless of
the absurdity of creating religious images only to destroy them – or
destroying religious images only to re-make them – there are important
implications linked to this apparently fruitless process. In order to
investigate these and other aspects of Emily Pfeiffer's poetry, I shall
principally concentrate on the works published between 1873 and
1884. During these years, pressured by her allegiance to the rapidly
growing women's movement, Pfeiffer was driven to re-imagine
aspects of her faith in ways compatible with her emancipationist
values. The result of this conflict was the creation of a series of poems
and poetic works that prove her to be a highly original and prescient late-
Victorian religious poet.

During the Victorian period a growing number of women poets were
starting to encroach upon territory that had hitherto been considered
a male preserve. Traditionally only male poets – men endowed with
special spiritual gifts – were deemed wise enough to penetrate divine
mysteries and make them known to ordinary people. In his lecture
'The Hero as Poet', Thomas Carlyle referred to these men as the '*Vates*

9

Prophets', a title that not only embraced the great men of literature – men like Dante or Shakespeare – but also the man Carlyle described as possessing 'the highest Voice ever heard on this earth [who said] "Consider the lilies of the field; they toil not, neither do they spin: yet Solomon in all his glory was not arrayed like one of these".'[1] In his subsequent lecture, 'The Hero as Priest', Carlyle drew attention to the fact that throughout history 'Theories of Life worthy to be sung by a Dante, Practices of Life by a Shakespeare . . . [had] given place to the fierce lightning of the Reformer'.[2] Thus the *Vates* Prophet – the man granted visionary gifts by God – was 'the product and ultimate adjustment of Reform [and as such] a symptom of his epoch'.[3]

Carlyle acknowledged the ability of powerful reformers to influence the 'Theories' and 'Practices' of the *Vates* Prophets. One of the most powerful Reformers in this respect was the Emperor Constantine I who (c. 324 AD) made Christianity a state religion in order to augment the power of the Roman Empire. Not long afterwards fifty Bibles were produced for use in the churches of Constantinople. At the great Church Council of Nicaea (c. 325 AD), an early version of the Nicene Creed was constructed and priests were appointed as intermediaries between God and Man. In this way 'Jesus of Nazareth, a man approved of God among you by miracles and wonders and signs, which God did by him in the midst of you, as ye yourselves also know', was replaced by the theological Christ.[4]

In her publication, *Alpha and Omega* (1915), Jane Ellen Harrison (1850–1928) writes:

> I know I am apt not to be fair to theology. I owe it a sort of grudge, because the impossibility of accepting its man-made figments made me for years think I was irreligious, whereas I know myself by temperament to be deeply, perhaps almost insanely, religious. The unseen is always haunting me, surging up behind the visible – a positive weakness for the 'religion of Time', because things temporal are apt to go misty.[5]

Harrison finds it impossible to accept what she calls the 'man-made figments' of theology and yet professes to being 'deeply' religious. Haunted by the unseen, she emphasises the dichotomy that exists between theology and 'Time' on the one hand, and invisible, timeless forces on the other. For Harrison only the timeless, invisible experience is religious. From this perspective, when looking more closely at the history of the Church from around 324 AD onwards, it is hard not to be critical of the men who imposed theology upon religion. This imposition is encapsulated in the full title of *The Book of Common Prayer* (1844):

> The Book of Common Prayer, and administration of Sacraments and other Rites and Ceremonies according to the use of The United Church of England and Ireland together with the Psalter on Psalms of David, pointed as they are to be sung or said in churches; and the Form and Manner of Making, Ordaining, and Consecrating of Bishops, Priests, and Deacons.[6]

Priests trained to administer the sacraments also had the power to purify wives after childbirth because, unlike Christ, Christian babies were born in sin. Should an infant die before being baptised its soul would go to hell. Priests also controlled the marriage ceremony, a ritual during which the bride and groom had to vow to bring up their offspring according to doctrines prescribed by the priests – a practice guaranteed to ensure the on-going survival of the institution. Thus the Christian Church became the richest and most powerful institution in the world, with authority even over governments, kings, and nations. In contrast to the beauty of the churches and cathedrals, the musical works, and the poems, prayers, and hymns inspired by faith, there was ecclesiastical bigotry, fanaticism, and dogmatism. Many men and women (mostly women) believed to have supernatural gifts were burnt alive, while countless ordinary Christians lived in abject terror of hell-fire for committing minor acts that the Church deemed sinful.

Traditionally, women could not occupy the role of the *Vates* Prophet, nor could they be priests, and although many women wrote hymns and devotional poems during the nineteenth century, serious religious discourse was generally considered unsuited to the female mind. Yet in the 1870s and 1880s, Emily Pfeiffer not only wrote religious poems, in some of them she even adopted the role of the *Vates* Prophet in order to make her feminist points. A consummate versifier, Pfeiffer was able to incorporate a whole battery of devices into her work to divert critical attention from her more transgressive subtexts, while at the same time drawing attention to the plight of women in a changing world. During Pfeiffer's lifetime the Established Church was losing members not only to Nonconformism at one end of the Christian spectrum and Tractarianism and Roman Catholicism at the other, but also to non-Christian ideologies such as Theism and Atheism. The twin bombshells of Charles Darwin's great works, *On the Origin of Species by Means of Natural Selection* (1859) and *The Descent of Man and Selection in Relation to Sex* (1871), were throwing the old theological certainties up in the air. During these turbulent decades, members of the Victorian intelligentsia were hard-pressed to reassess values that they had taken for granted, while emancipationists were starting to question the authority of a biblical text that not only marginalised, but also misrepresented, women.

Today, looking back to the Victorian period, feminist theologians – women such as Rosemary Radford Ruether and Elisabeth Schüssler Fiorenza – readily acknowledge their debt to the nineteenth-century American emancipationist Elizabeth Cady Stanton (1815–1902), of whom Fiorenza writes:

> [Stanton] argued that it is important for women to interpret the Bible, because scripture and its authority have been and continue to be used against women struggling for emancipation. Moreover, women as well as men have internalized scripture's misogynist teachings as the Word of God. Hence, [Stanton] and her collaborators utilized historical-critical scholarship to argue that the Bible is the word of men who have projected their own selfish interests into it ... Since men have also been the Bible's authoritative interpreters throughout the centuries, she argued, women must now claim their right to biblical interpretation.[7]

Elizabeth Cady Stanton published *The Woman's Bible* (1895) to draw attention to ways the Bible contributed to the subordination of women. Stanton and her team of female scholars wanted to reinterpret and reconstruct those texts which they believed had been construed by men in ways that misrepresented or excluded women, and in this respect Stanton's Bible was an early example of modern-day feminist re-constructionist theology. In her introduction to *The Woman's Bible*, Stanton sets out her arguments:

> The Bible teaches that woman brought sin and death into the world, that she precipitated the fall of the race, that she

> was arraigned before the judgment seat of Heaven, tried,
> condemned and sentenced. Marriage for her was to be a
> condition of bondage . . . and in silence and subjection she
> was to play the role of a dependent on man's bounty . . .[8]

Stanton draws attention to the hypocrisy of a Church which allows women to be its chief supporter but uses its power to make emancipation impossible. She concludes her introduction by stating that 'the most bitter outspoken enemies of woman are found among clergymen and bishops of the Protestant religion'.[9] Canon law, creeds, scriptures, and religions, Stanton believes, bear the hallmarks of 'fallible man', and not the 'Spirit of all Good' around which everything in the universe rotates.

While some Victorian feminists were leaving the Established Church to join other Christian sects and denominations, or losing their faith altogether, others were becoming increasingly interested in paganism, as Margot K. Louis explains:

> Interest in goddesses generally revived in the nineteenth
> century, thanks to the cultural shifts created by Romanticism,
> and thanks also to the work of scholars like Johann Jakob
> Bachofen, whose book *Das Mutterrecht* (1861) proposed
> that patriarchal society must have been preceded by matri-
> archy . . .[10] Moreover, the gradual collapse of religious faith
> in the nineteenth century was intimately connected with the
> development of fresh intellectual and emotional approaches
> to death, resurrection, and mythic thinking itself. The slow,
> difficult alteration in the position of women also prompted
> new ways of thinking about violation, marriage, and the
> relationship of mother and daughter. All these changes were
> reflected and explored in the literature that employs the myth
> of Persephone.[11]

Religious uncertainty also contributed to a revival of magic which became focused on the Hermetic Order of the Golden Dawn, an order founded in 1888. Aspects of this order, thought to be the single greatest influence of twentieth-century occultism, formed the core of neo-paganism, which grew in popularity during the First World War and proliferated following the repeal of the Witchcraft Act in 1951. Since then an increasing number of women have left the Church of England to join neo-pagan religions. In 2008 an article published in the

Daily Telegraph reported that more than a million women had left the Established Church during the previous ten years. Apparently as many as 50,000 British women were leaving the Church annually because they did not 'feel as included in the Church as men'.[12] In the same article, sociologist Dr Kristin Aune explained that 'young women . . . dislike the traditionalism and hierarchies they imagine are integral to the Church'.[13] Aune's statistics suggest that many women were leaving the Church in order to become neo-pagans because, as pagans, they could exert a degree of power. Aune's research appeared in *Women and Religion in the West* (2008), in which her co-editor, Giselle Vincett, published her article 'The Fusers: New Forms of Spiritualized Christianity'.[14] Vincett's absorbing essay draws attention to Christian 'fusers' – Christian feminists who incorporate elements of neo-paganism into their personal belief-systems. 'Disaffected by the Church', she writes, these women 'question authority and hierarchy [and] are further united by their feminism, which drives their spirituality in their need to find ways of imagining the divine that are consistent with their feminine values'.[15]

Bearing all these issues, events, and trends in mind, my starting point for the pages that follow is the question, where, if anywhere, does Emily Pfeiffer's poetry fit into this complex picture? In order to try to supply answers to this question, I begin my investigation into Pfeiffer's poetry by commenting on a lyric tradition established by Laetitia Landon and Felicia Hemans earlier in the nineteenth century. Demonstrating Pfeiffer's adherence to this tradition in her poem 'Gerard's Monument' (1873), I show her subverting this mode in her love-lyric 'Everild' (1876).

In Chapter One, I also consider the yardstick I should adopt when evaluating Pfeiffer's poetry, now that the criteria for what constitutes religious poetry have changed. Today it is understood that religious debate was almost inseparable from politics, science, and other key issues that concerned the Victorians, and that this should be reflected in interpretations of nineteenth-century poetry.[16] Before applying these criteria to my interpretations of Pfeiffer's poetry, however, I first compare Emily Pfeiffer's religious background with that of Elizabeth Barrett Browning, before briefly assessing religious poems by Dora Greenwell and Anna Letitia Waring through the eyes of a critic writing for *Contemporary Review* in 1869.

The first lyric poem that I investigate, published in 1873, is unusual for Pfeiffer because it leans towards a religious literary convention that came to dominate devotional and religious poetry in the nineteenth century. Later, in her lyric poem 'The Crown of Song' (1876), Pfeiffer moves away from this convention when she tackles a range of feminist issues relating to the spiritual demise of a dead woman poet waiting outside the gates of heaven. In her 'Hymn to the Dark Christmas of 1874' (1876) Pfeiffer uses a train crash as an allegory for loss of faith, and foresees terrible consequences for the future of Christianity. The two sonnets I discuss here show Pfeiffer exploiting evolutionary theory by attaching what she sees as women's moral and religious superiority to the evolutionary concept of adaptation, change, and progress.

My second chapter draws upon Emily Pfeiffer's treatment of topics popular with women poets during the nineteenth century – Women and Nature; Women and the Virgin Mother; and Fallen Women. Written in the 1870s and 1880s, when the women's movement was growing fast, these poems show Pfeiffer trying to reconcile her feminist values with her Christian faith. In a short elegy called 'A Song of Winter' (1879) Pfeiffer elevates the spiritual status of women by linking their stigmatisation to Jesus' crucifixion and resurrection. In a notably less conventional ballad, 'Madonna Dūnya' (1879), Pfeiffer exploits the iconography of the Virgin and Child in order to present an image of motherhood that transcends male-inscribed limitations. In submitting this important poem to critical discussion, I support my argument that Pfeiffer may have enjoyed greater freedom to express her religious ideas than many of her female contemporaries. In 'From Out of the Night' (1882), an epic romance which takes the form of a lamenting soliloquy, or 'Complaint', a young girl reflects on the details of her passionate love affair and subsequent betrayal before committing suicide. In this poem Pfeiffer uses the 'fallen woman' theme to draw attention to issues that cause the young girl to reject her Christian faith.

Pfeiffer's Welsh-inspired blank-verse novel, *Glân-Alarch, His Silence and Song* (1877), a publication for which there appears to be no poetic equivalent amongst Pfeiffer's female contemporaries, is the subject of Chapter Three. In this verse novel, published two years before the publication of 'Madonna Dūnya', Pfeiffer's emancipationist values come into direct conflict with her Christian belief-system.

Using poetic devices to protect herself from censure, Pfeiffer sets her novel within a period of pre-history about which little is known. Then she appropriates and exploits a series of mythical figures which she weaves into her narrative for her own feminist purposes. She then takes her readers on a paper-chase up and around the mountains of North Wales, superimposing her own version of sixth-century religious imagery upon a nineteenth-century Christian template. Unaware of subsequent discoveries about the leadership of Jesus' disciple, Mary Magdalene, Pfeiffer nevertheless creates a mythology centred upon an iconic woman leader with supernatural gifts. Re-articulating legend and folk-tale in a manner consistent with a period in history when the real and fantastical, the past and present intertwined, Pfeiffer can be considered an early exponent of 'mythopoeia'. Providing two explanations for the survival of her 'fallen' heroine – one natural and one supernatural – Pfeiffer provides an opportunity for *Glân-Alarch* to be read as a feminist proto-allegory of the Christian myth.

In my fourth and final chapter, I present an extended commentary on *The Rhyme of the Lady of the Rock, and How it Grew* (1884), an experimental mixed-genre work that operates on several different levels. In this extraordinarily sophisticated double narrative, a Victorian poet visiting the Scottish island of Mull writes a folk-ballad about a crime that took place in medieval times. Having written what she believes to be the definitive account of this atrocity, the poet's husband reads the ballad to a group of auditors. In comparing events in the Victorian prose frame narrative with the events in the medieval Scottish folk-ballad, I comment on important aspects relating to the construction and transmission of each. Superficially, *The Rhyme of the Lady of the Rock, and How it Grew* remains a fascinating travelogue, as well as a good read, but its multi-layered subtexts are subtle and complex. This publication may well be Pfeiffer's most challenging religious work.

The ubiquity of religious themes in Victorian poetry makes it more difficult, yet more imperative, to appreciate the originality of Emily Pfeiffer's religious poetry. Elizabeth Gray suggests that Victorian women poets sometimes 'present and invite new views of the [biblical] canon': so how, if at all, does Pfeiffer accomplish this in the context of new definitions of what constitutes religious poetry?[17]

INTRODUCTION

Today, in the twenty-first century, the Established Church is generally more tolerant of religious diversity than it was in the past, and this and other relevant factors need to be taken into account when assessing Pfeiffer's religious verse. It is in the light of such criteria that I shall seek to argue that the series of poems Emily Pfeiffer wrote and published between 1873 and 1884 – so diverse in form and subject, so skilful in technique, and so sustained in close thought – demonstrates her self-evident position as an innovative and prescient religious poet.

Notes

1. Thomas Carlyle, *On Heroes and Hero-worship and the Heroic in History* (London: George Routledge & Sons, Ltd., [1840]), p. 109.

2. Ibid., p. 156.

3. Ibid.

4. Acts 2:22.

5. Jane Ellen Harrison, *Alpha and Omega* (London: Sidgwick & Jackson Ltd, 1915), pp. 206–7.

6. *Book of Common Prayer* (London: George E. Eyre and Andrew Spottiswoode, 1844).

7. Elisabeth Schüssler Fiorenza, ed., *Searching the Scriptures: Feminist Commentary*, 2 vols (New York: Herder & Herder, 1994), 2, 1 (Introduction).

8. Elizabeth Cady Stanton, ed. *The Woman's Bible: Pentateuch*, 2 vols (New York: European Publishing Co., 1895), 1, 7 (Introduction).

9. Ibid., p. 13.

10. See J. J. Bachofen, *Myth, Religion, and Mother Right*, trans. Ralph Manheim (Princeton: Princeton University Press, 1982).

11. Margot K. Louis, *Persephone Rises, 1860–1927: Mythography, Gender, and the Creation of a New Spirituality* (Farnham, Surrey: Ashgate, 2009), Preface, p. ix.

12. Martin Beckford, 'Religious Affairs', *Daily Telegraph*, 23 August, 2008, 13.

13. Ibid.

14. Kristin Aune, Sonya Sharma, and Giselle Vincett, eds., *Women and Religion in the West: Challenging Secularization* (Aldershot: Ashgate, 2008), p. 133.

15. Ibid., p. 136.

16. Mark Knight and Emma Mason, *Nineteenth-Century Religion and Literature: Introduction* (Oxford: Oxford University Press, 2006), p. 3.

17. Elizabeth Gray, *The Christian and Lyric Tradition in Victorian Women's Poetry* (London: Routledge, 2010), p. 40.

CHAPTER ONE

Writing Against the Bias

E MILY PFEIFFER was a late-Victorian poet who, during the 1870s and 1880s, found her emancipationist values becoming increasingly incompatible with aspects of her Christian faith. In the eleven years between 1873 and 1884 she wrote poems and poetic works which reflect this growing conflict, and it is the aim of this study to identify and evaluate some of these changes in her religious verse. In this chapter, I start by evaluating Pfeiffer's poetry against criteria that have, traditionally, defined the lyric genre.

In her early lyric poetry Pfeiffer appears to be a proponent of what Isobel Armstrong has called 'the poetics of expression',[1] as exemplified in the following extract from the title poem of *Gerard's Monument and Other Poems* (1873):

> And sometimes when his sister came
>   Bringing the morning in her hair,
> And in her eyes the pure soft flame
>   Of human love, and cleared the air
> Of thick night-fancies with her breath,
>   And with her hands' cool pressure chased
>   The vagrant thoughts which burn to waste, –
> So with quick life abashing death, –
> Those tears of lonely anguish yet
> On Gerard's wasted cheek were wet.[2]

In expressing 'the pure soft flame / Of human love', the 'cool pressure' of hands, the 'vagrant thoughts', the 'tears of lonely anguish', and the 'wasted cheek', Pfeiffer is ostensibly all gush and feeling.

19

Conforming to, or confined to, a women's tradition set in train by poets such as Laetitia Landon ('L.E.L.') (1802–38) and Felicia Hemans (1793–1835), 'Gerard's Monument' is redolent of qualities that have tended to make Victorian women's lyric poetry the butt of adverse scholarly criticism. William Rossetti's 'Prefatory Notice' for a posthumous edition of Felicia Hemans's poetry, probably published in 1873 (the same year as *Gerard's Monument* itself), typifies this kind of criticism:

> Her skill, however, hardly rises into the loftier region of art . . . Her sources of inspiration being genuine, and tone of her mind feminine in an intense degree, the product has no lack of sincerity: and yet it leaves a certain artificial impression, rather perhaps through a cloying flow of 'right-minded' perceptions of moral and material beauty . . . One might sum up the weak points in Mrs. Hemans's poetry by saying that it is not only 'feminine' poetry . . . but also 'female' poetry: besides exhibiting the fineness and charm of womanhood, it has the monotone of mere sex.[3]

According to Armstrong, Rossetti's use of such terms as the 'feminine' mind, the 'cloying flow' of 'female' poetry, and 'the monotone of mere sex' was a typical response by men who felt uneasy about women writing lyric poetry.[4] The same unease can be seen in the terms adopted by the anonymous reviewer of Pfeiffer's collection in the *Pall Mall Gazette*:[5]

> Her love lyrics are, with one or two exceptions, sentimental and feeble, unmusical in form and sickly in thought. The volume opens with two poems of this description. The first contains some good lines, and is only occasionally ridiculous; but the second, called 'Everild', belongs to the 'Laura Matilda' school of poetry . . . Mrs. Pfeiffer is by no means strong in the lyric. Her ear plays her false, and she lacks the sense of fitness which imperceptibly but surely guides the lyric poet on the right way . . .

Using the terms 'sentimental', 'feeble', 'unmusical' and 'sickly' in his critique of Pfeiffer's lyric poetry, the critic singles out the love-lyric 'Everild' as being especially 'ridiculous'. In this poem the speaker addresses a rose, but it is only in the fourth and final stanza that it transpires that the 'rose' is actually Everild, the speaker's wife.

The third and fourth stanzas read as follows:

> O symbol Rose with fragrant heart!
> It was not thus in halcyon days
> You had not these sweet hidden ways,
> Your single beauty open'd wide,
> It had not learnt this tender pride,
> Nor knew from an exhaustless mine
> To make each yielded gift divine!
>
> My blushing, close-lipped Everild!
> Your heart is secret as the rose,
> Whose guarded treasure still o'er flows
> Upon the air, and makes a sphere
> Precious to all who linger near.
> For me that heart, my sphinx, my wife,
> Holds revelations deep as life![6]

A husband expresses his love for his wife and, superficially at least, Pfeiffer's love-lyric conforms to the conventions of the genre. Yet Pfeiffer's narrative voice uses a husband to make inferences about his wife in ways that the reviewer of the *Pall Mall Gazette* either objected to or missed completely. The first point that Pfeiffer makes through the husband speaker is that the wife, Everild, has secrets – 'nectar' and 'covert bliss' – which she hides within herself. Secondly, Pfeiffer's male speaker suggests that these secret treasures pertain to a 'mystic wealth' locked deep within her heart. No boastful male invader can ravish Everild in order to obtain the sacred riches she conceals. Holding within herself 'revelations deep as life', Everild has learned to guard her treasure, her 'gift divine'. Beneath this outpouring of romantic love a subtext emerges. The love-object, Everild, who in more halcyon days had been open and trusting, has now learned to be silent. The 'gift' of secrecy makes her ever more mysterious, mystical, desirable, and precious to her husband and, because of her silence, he can more fully express his feelings. The darker side of this poem, relating to what Armstrong describes as 'the aesthetics of the secret', suggests that what the husband sees as 'mystic wealth' and 'covert bliss' is not the case.[7] Marriage for Everild has been a slow process of repression. What Everild's husband sees as sphinx-like and secretive could in fact be symptoms of depression, or neurasthenia. Far from being 'ridiculous', Pfeiffer's poem can be seen as a mid-to-late-Victorian version of a lyric tradition established by poets such as Anne and Emily Brontë, Adelaide Procter, Dora Greenwell, and others. While outwardly conforming to the conventions of the genre, there is that inner voice which for Greenwell is 'so sad, so truthful, so earnest, that we have felt as if some intimate secret were at once communicated and withheld'.[8]

There is, of course, another way of reading this poem, and one that ties in with views Pfeiffer expressed in a prose work published in the early years of her marriage. In *Valisneria, or A Midsummer Day's Dream* (1857), a wife takes the moral high-ground when she teaches her husband to practise the Christian message of charity.[9] Conforming to his wife's expectations of him, the husband calls his wife 'true guardian spirit and prophetess', and readily acknowledges her right, even her prerogative as a wife, to guide him towards a virtuous lifestyle. In 'Everild' the husband makes similar points as he addresses his wife. Referring to secret treasures – 'hoarded gifts' and 'mystic wealth' – the husband acknowledges the sacred knowledge and wisdom his wife has acquired and stored up within herself during their marriage. Although Everild's spirituality, her 'guarded treasure', is held deep within her heart, 'all who linger near' find themselves in a sphere made precious by her divine gifts. In this interpretation of 'Everild', Pfeiffer, writing later in the century, inverts 'the aesthetics of the secret'. Far from being a sad, silent, and repressed sexual object, Everild is a 'revelation', a power-house of spirituality. Pfeiffer conforms to 'the aesthetics of the secret' in order to subvert it by portraying Everild, a wife, as the strong, spiritually dominant, silent, sphinx-like partner in her marriage. All the feminine gush is manifested by the husband – the gender roles reversed.

That the reviewer for the *Pall Mall Gazette* failed to appreciate the subtlety of 'Everild' is the starting point for my exposition of Pfeiffer's religious verse. But first I need to make the point that as a middle-of-the-road – or central – Protestant, Pfeiffer is a rarity in terms of her late-Victorian female contemporaries. Although her literary milieu included Atheists, Theists, Baptists, Methodists, Wesleyans, Congregationalists, Tractarians, Quakers, Unitarians, Presbyterians, Roman Catholics, Swedenborgians, and Hylo-Idealists, where (apart from a small number of hymn-writers) are her late-Victorian female central Protestant contemporaries?[10] Another important point is that, bearing in mind the broad diversity of nineteenth-century religious belief in general, and

Christian belief in particular, the canon of Victorian 'religious' verse was until recent years deemed to be represented by – and defined by – the religious values of one literary mode. Looking back to earlier in the nineteenth century, I shall now consider the influence of John Keble (1792–1866) and High Church doctrine on the canon of Victorian religious poetry.

During the nineteenth century John Keble's hugely popular book of devotional poems, *The Christian Year* (1827), was read by great swathes of British Christians. In 1833, Keble founded the Oxford movement with John Newman (1801–90) and Edward Pusey (1800–82) with the aim of breathing new life into the Anglican Church by reviving the authority of the Church's Founding Fathers. Keble, Newman, and other Oxford clergymen published a series of Tracts between 1833 and 1841 setting out the tenets of the movement. 'Tract 90', written by Newman in 1841, suggested that the Thirty-Nine Articles of religion in *The Book of Common Prayer* were to some extent compatible with Roman Catholic doctrine. Four years later, Newman converted to the Roman Catholic Church and the movement came to a close, and yet the influence of 'Tractarianism' remained far-reaching. In 1831, Keble had been elected Professor of Poetry at Oxford, and had become an authority on poetry which he saw as 'a kind of medicine divinely bestowed upon man, which gives healing relief to mental emotion, yet without detriment to modest reserve'.[11] Keble, endorsing Thomas Carlyle's idea of the poet as the *Vates* – in the sense that he saw poetry as 'divinely bestowed upon man' – also saw poetry as a safe outlet for relieving the pent-up emotions of the Christian *Vates* himself.

Later, in 1861, *Hymns Ancient & Modern* (*A&M*) was published, and the compilers of the hymnal strived to ensure that it represented the full spectrum of Protestantism. John Keble himself took an active part in *A&M*'s construction. In 1869 *A&M* (which Lowther Clarke describes as 'avowedly Tractarian') had been in circulation for eight years.[12] By then Keble had been dead for three years, but nevertheless the Tractarian mode was already coming to represent religious and devotional poetry as a whole.[13] In her essay ' "Her Silence Speaks": Keble's Female Heirs', Emma Mason draws attention to the way Keble's views on poetry became important to a group of nineteenth-century women poets:

[Keble's] shaping of an at once restrained and intensely emotional poetics is nevertheless fundamentally central to the poetry of several nineteenth-century women poets – Dora Greenwell, Cecil Frances Alexander, Caroline Leakey, Bessie Parkes, Adelaide Anne Procter – wary of their assumed proclivity to extreme sentimentalism.[14]

'The close connection between devotional poetry and hymnody,' states G. B. Tennyson, 'is made clear by the extent to which Tractarian devotional poetry stimulated a whole new development in hymnody and modified even the well-established Evangelical tradition.'[15] There were Victorians, however, who were not happy with this tendency. In his article for *Contemporary Review* (1869), H. A. Page criticises 'the ascetic order of religious literature' which he describes as 'self-conscious' and 'reactionary'. In his view, more spontaneous expressions of faith were needed to combat the threats to Christianity from science and higher criticism:[16]

> There is an atmosphere of selectness, if we may name it so, about their poetry . . . There is an esoteric and an exoteric teaching wrapped up in their song . . . The gist of the whole matter seems to be this: that so long as earnest religious convictions are covertly assailed by science and criticism, we shall have plenty of true religious poetry, but little of the very highest kind, because this is only possible where the poet sings spontaneously and in the full consciousness of giving utterance to homogeneous, unimpaired beliefs, or at all events, beliefs which have either not yet been cast into the alembic of science, or have fully emerged from it, clearer, brighter, and more firmly established than ever. We have full hope that the truths of Christianity, so far as they have been imperilled by science, will triumphantly emerge, and therefore we wait expectantly.[17]

After criticising Frances Havergal's publication *The Ministry of Song* (1862), Page lambasts Dora Greenwell's poetic work, *Carmina Crucis* (1869). A supporter of women's emancipation, Greenwell (1821–82) was not a sectarian Christian and it is thought that she may even have joined the Society of Friends after the death of her mother.[18] Her devotional poetry, however, is generally High Anglican in tone and the deeply religious poems in *Carmina Crucis* express intense compassion. Consider the first two of the seven stanzas of 'Schola Crucis, Schola Lucis' quoted by Page:

Beneath thy cross I stand,
    Jesus, my Saviour, turn and look on me;
Oh! Who are these that, one on either hand,
    Are crucified with Thee?

The one that turns away,
    With sullen, scoffing lip, – and one whose eyes
Close o'er the words, 'Yet shalt thou be this day
    With me in paradise . . .'[19]

Of these stanzas Page writes: 'We have here a simplicity quite out of harmony with the subtlety of feeling and idea which the poem seeks to express, and the result will inevitably be that where the idea is caught, a sense of dissatisfaction with the form . . . will be felt.' Yet he praises the hymns of Anna Letitia Waring, writing:

> Miss Waring stands almost at the opposite pole from Miss Greenwell. She is one of the few hymn writers who maintain, amid the criticism and doubt of our day, much of the sweet unconsciousness and subdued warmth of earlier singers. There is a quiet, self-sufficient fervour about her poems, and a pellucid flow of verse, which is the result neither of art nor polish, but seems to flow, like a spring, crystal-clear . . .[20]

Page then quotes Waring's hymn 'My heart is resting, O my God', the first stanza of which reads:

> Sometimes I long for promised bliss,
>   But it will not come too late –
> And the songs of patient spirits rise
>   From the place wherein I wait;
> While in the faith that makes no haste
>   My soul has time to see
> A kneeling host of Thy redeemed,
>   In fellowship with me.[21]

Then Page conflates what he sees as the two poets' religious and poetic stances: whereas Dora Greenwell's poetry is 'Catholic and conventional', A. L. Waring's hymns are 'open air and Protestant'. Then, near the end of his article, he overtly denigrates Keble and his religious convictions:

> It is only to be expected that the work of restoring and confirming a too sorely-tried faith by hymns and psalms and spiritual songs should be most successfully done by women or by feminine natures. John Keble had a dash of the

feminine temperament . . . [and] was most decided – strong-
headed even – in his opposition to anything that in the least
threatened his own cherished convictions; but his firmness
was not that of well-reasoned, tolerant, masculine assurance,
but partook rather of the querulous, exclusive self-sufficiency
of a delicate feminine organization.[22]

Seeing Keble and his 'female heirs' as too delicate, too reactionary, and
too self-conscious to take on the challenges of secularism and scientific
criticism, what Page wants, he writes, is strong, manly religious poetry
– poetry that speaks to all Christians, not just to 'feminine' Tractarians:

While the knights rode out, redressing human wrongs, and
punishing those who had done cruelly or dishonestly, the
maidens sang songs, embroidered emblems, or executed
sacred illuminations; so now, while the stronger members are
doing battle with the enemy on his own ground, investigating
the scientific bulwarks, and counter-working underground, the
gentler ones are re-beautifying the sanctuary and raising new
songs of hope and exultation as they go through the glorious
work . . .[23]

H. A. Page resented the 'Catholic and conventional' poetics of Keble's
'female heirs', preferring the 'open air and Protestant' verse of women
like the hymn-writer A. L. Waring. But there was another 'open air and
Protestant' poet out in the field of battle, fighting to 'redress human
wrongs': her name was Emily Pfeiffer. Yet in her untitled poem which
starts with the words 'He that is washed needs but to wash his feet',
taken from St John's Gospel, Pfeiffer conforms to the High Church
definition of the religious poem.[24]

'HE THAT IS WASHED NEEDS BUT TO WASH HIS FEET' (1873)

Although I argue that each of the poems by Emily Pfeiffer that I evaluate
in this book is religious, this is the only poem that leans towards
conventions that, until recently, defined the canon of Victorian religious
poetry. Taken from the New Testament, Pfeiffer supplies Christ's words
as recorded in John 13:10 in lieu of a title: 'He that is washed needeth
not save to wash his feet, but is clean every whit'.[25]

This short lyric poem, consisting of three six-line stanzas, refers to
the part in St John's Gospel where Jesus, knowing that he will soon

be killed, undresses, wraps himself in a towel, and pours water into a basin. Then he washes his disciples' feet. When he comes to wash Simon Peter's feet, the disciple is distressed to see his Lord demean himself in this way, but Jesus says: 'If I wash thee not, thou hast no part with me'.[26] Simon Peter then says to Jesus: 'Lord, not my feet only, but also my hands and my head'.[27] Jesus answers, saying: 'He that is washed needeth not save to wash his feet, but is clean every whit':[28] Pfeiffer considers Jesus' words:

> He that is washed needs but to wash his feet,
>   And he is wholly clean. What words are these
> So hard, so dark, they warn us from the heat
>   Of outward sense, and bid us rise to seize
> Some ray of light flashed downwards from the sun
> Of truth, eternal as the truthful One.
>
> He that is washed needs but to wash his feet;
>   His comings and his goings must be clean,
> His path still pure adown life's crowded street,
>   His track upon its mire and slime unseen.
> Few are too weak or vile to purge their walk;
> Our Master did not mock us in His talk.
>
> He bade us do the thing we could – no more;
>   Be heedful of our outward ways and deeds.
> Watch well our feet – that so He might outpour
>   His spirit for our spirits' inward needs:
> Till we in Sabbath rest and peace should sit,
> And hear His words, 'Clean are ye every whit'.

Pfeiffer's initial question ('What words are these?') seems strangely redundant, since Jesus Himself explains the symbolism behind his actions in John 13:13–18:

> Ye call me Master and Lord: and ye say well; for so I am.
>   If I then, your Lord and Master, have washed your feet; ye also ought to wash one another's feet.
>   For I have given you an example, that ye should do as I have done to you.
>   Verily, verily, I say unto you, the servant is not greater than his lord; neither is he that is sent greater than he that sent him.
>   If ye know these things, happy are ye if ye do them.
>   I speak not of you all: I know whom I have chosen: but that the scripture may be fulfilled.

Despite this, Pfeiffer provides her own interpretation of Jesus' words, explaining the difference between two types of cleanliness: bodily cleanliness is one thing, spiritual cleanliness is another. Those who are spiritually clean because they have been cleansed by the Holy Spirit remain pure, leaving no track of sinfulness upon the crowded, slimy, and muddy path of life. If the spirit is pure we do not have to worry about the things we cannot do: all we have to do is to worry about what we can do – the external, physical things. Our inner spiritual needs are looked after by God who pours His spirit into us; thus, when in worshipful repose and meditation, we hear His words of comfort: 'Clean are ye every whit'.

Unusually for Pfeiffer, this lyric poem lacks a clear feminist subtext. Pfeiffer simply explores Jesus' words in the Gospel and gives her interpretation of the text to her readers. Though clearly a religious poem, it nevertheless lacks the rarefied religious intensity of the Tractarian mode that, as G. B. Tennyson observes, 'modified the Evangelical tradition' during the Victorian period. Yet nor does it conform to the 'open air and Protestant' style of A. L. Waring's hymnody. In the next poem that I investigate Pfeiffer diverges from the criteria that, until recently, were used to define nineteenth-century religious poetry.

'THE CROWN OF SONG' (1876) [29]

'The Crown of Song' consists of thirty-three four-line stanzas supposedly narrated by a woman poet who, because of her clairvoyant and clairaudient powers, is able to tap into the psychic pain of a dead poet waiting outside the gates of heaven. This first poet describes how, by folding back her sensory receptors, she is able to engage her 'inner eye' to follow events occurring in the spirit world. In describing this process, the visionary poet uses words similar to those Elizabeth Barrett Browning had used thirty years earlier in her poem 'Human Life's Mystery'.[30] In Barrett Browning's poem the narrator refers to 'the senses folding thick and dark / About the stifled soul within, / We guess diviner things beyond' – words that suggest that Pfeiffer may have been influenced by this work. Yet, while it is tempting to compare the two poets' work, it has to be remembered that they were raised in different religious environments – Barrett Browning as a Congregationalist and Pfeiffer as a central Anglican. And even if their religious experience changed, or even converged, during the course of their lives, their early religious conditioning would ultimately separate them on essential matters of doctrine; Barrett Browning, moreover, was not a late-Victorian poet. Karen Dieleman nevertheless points out difficulties that would have been shared by both poets:

> Only male poets and prose writers could claim the visionary authority of an Old Testament prophet to critique Victorian culture and offer alternative world views. The ideological configurations of respectable femininity also discouraged women writers from participating in such public and authoritative discourse.[31]

In her description of sage discourse, Dieleman draws attention to Thaïs Morgan's view that Victorian women writers often critiqued and subverted the patriarchal model of the form by boldly entering 'the masculine world of socio-economic conflict, theological polemic, and sexual politics', despite the risks associated with 'adopting a "masculine" tone of authority'.[32] Referring to those who see *Aurora Leigh* as an example of sage discourse (or Victorian Nonconformist sage discourse), Dieleman argues that 'the poet-as-prophet paradigm was actually a conflicted one for Barrett Browning'.[33] Firstly, Dieleman argues, 'the figure of a cultural prophet imbued with authoritative vision revealed to him alone . . . did not ultimately accord with Barrett Browning's democratic attitude as to how [religious] knowledge or wisdom is gained'.[34] Dieleman explains that in the Congregationalist Declaration of Faith, 'human traditions, fathers and councils, canons and creeds, possess no authority of the faith and practice of Christians'.[35] While Congregationalist preachers had to earn the respect of both sexes, 'preachers and priests in the Church of England and in the Roman Catholic Church were seen as the inheritors of apostolic authority'.[36] Dieleman goes on to suggest that only late in her career, in *Aurora Leigh*, was Barrett Browning able to overcome her egalitarian Congregationalist principles and represent a woman as a poet-preacher.

Not so Pfeiffer. As a central Anglican, she had no difficulty in assuming for herself, and for the women represented in her poems, 'the figure of a cultural prophet imbued with authoritative vision revealed to [her] alone' in order to make religious statements.[37] To set out her own authoritative vision was less conflicted for Pfeiffer than it was for Barrett Browning.

Shortly after the publication of *Aurora Leigh* (1856), when Barrett Browning reversed the Victorian domestic status quo by depicting Romney as caring for the poor while Aurora wrote poetry, Pfeiffer published a prose fairy tale, *Valisneria, or A Midsummer Day's Dream* (1857), in which a wife says to her husband:

> I would have you employ your energies and talents in a way which might be acceptable to your Creator, and bring you the applause of your own conscience . . . In order that you might love me, I would have you love mankind . . .[38]

What Barrett Browning achieved with difficulty in her last years inspired Pfeiffer in her early years, and there was no doctrinal or ideological barrier holding Pfeiffer back from sage discourse. If, late in life, Barrett Browning came to feel that her classical education, her translations, and her renown as a poet, justified her characterisation of Aurora as the *Vates*, Pfeiffer had no such scruples.

In 'The Crown of Song' Pfeiffer challenges the 'poet-as-prophet paradigm' referred to by Dieleman as being a male figure 'imbued with authoritative vision revealed to him alone'.[39] By deploying a woman poet visionary as her speaker, Pfeiffer directly opposes the traditional viewpoint consolidated by the words of Thomas Carlyle in 1840, that 'the *Vates*, whether Prophet or Poet . . . is a man sent hither to make [divine mystery] more impressively known to us'.[40] In this lyric poem Pfeiffer's *Vates* Poet is a *woman* who uses *her* 'authoritative vision' to make divine mystery more impressively known to us.

The poet narrator – the visionary who is able to access events occurring outside the gates of heaven – realises that the dead woman poet, the subject of her visions, has become fractured or dislocated in some way. Pfeiffer's visionary speaker uses the metaphor of a 'wayward bud' to describe this sense of disconnection (p. 40):

> I heard the sigh, and my tuneful heart
> Beat out the melody underneath,
> For the sigh was a sigh of itself, apart,
> As a wayward bud that has slipt its sheath.

Later in the poem, Pfeiffer links the metaphor of the 'wayward bud that has slipt its sheath' to that of 'deflower'd roses' (p. 44).

Hers was the sigh which had tuned my heart
To the sweet sad melody underneath;
A music beyond the reach of art,
As a wayward bud that has burst its sheath;

Hers was the only brow of the band
That, fair and stately, was still undower'd;
And I look'd, and saw in her drooping hand
A crown of roses, but all deflower'd.

In Victorian representations of women, the words 'wayward' and 'deflower'd' suggest transgressive, immoral behaviours to which the word 'undower'd' is the natural consequence; the wayward woman who becomes deflowered must remain 'undower'd'. In this context, however, Pfeiffer's metaphors 'wayward bud' and 'deflower'd rose' describe separation and death. Like embryos cut off from their sources of nourishment in the womb, or babies deprived their mothers' milk, detached buds and cut roses are destined to die. These bleak images suggest that the dead poet's spirit has become split off from its source of life, so she must die. But as the poet is already dead, these metaphors can only be referring to spiritual death. Pfeiffer seems to be implying that, for her waywardness, the dead poet's soul must be denied eternal life – a terrifying possibility which could explain the poet's repeated failure to respond when the seraphs call out her name. Eventually, she cries out in agony (p. 44):

Till at the last her passion broke,
Cleaving her lips with a tongue like flame;
'My work', she wail'd, is evanish'd as smoke,
My crown deperish'd, I have no name!'

Pfeiffer's use of prefixes ('undower'd', 'deflower'd', 'evanish'd', 'deperish'd') emphasise the ways Victorian women tended to be sub-defined by prefixed masculine codes. Her work has vanished, her crown has perished, and now her very soul must die. Heaven is barred to her (p. 47):

But her voice flew up as a bird, still higher,
'No calm, cold Priestess of Art, was I,
But a victim, slain in its sacred fire,
And all – to my very name – shall die!'

Everything has been taken from her – her name, her work, and her hopes of heaven; she is a victim slain in Art's sacred fire. For breaking a sacred code, for audaciously participating in sage discourse, for penetrating sacred mysteries accessible only to the *Vates* Prophet or Poet she – a woman – must forfeit eternal life. Thus, having been betrayed by patriarchy during her earthly existence, the dead poet must now suffer eternally for her waywardness. For how can she hope to enter a heaven controlled by patriarchs whose sacerdotal doctrines contributed to her marginalisation in the first place? Pfeiffer importantly addresses these points in the latter part of her poem.

When the souls waiting outside the gates of heaven hear the dead poet cry out, some of the male spirits recognise her as the author of the poetry that had helped them when they were alive. These eminent men – including a 'Patriot', a 'Doubter' and a 'Thinker' – all have good reason to remember the dead woman's poetry with gratitude. Each soul recognises the poet as the author of poems that had supported him through a particular crisis during his lifetime. She was the poet who had helped each man to attain his personal goal – whether through the attainment of clearer vision, selfless sacrifice, greater courage, or higher aspirations. Each man salutes her service to mankind. Finally, one of these men carries the poet in through the gates of heaven and deposits her at the foot of God's throne. In the silence she listens to a voice that thrills her heart (p. 48):

> There was silence. It thrill'd through the Singer's heart:
>   'Sink earthly fame in the earthly sod,
> Take thou with the martyr and saint thy part;
>   Who dies to himself, best lives to God.'
>
> Kneeling, she dropt the faded flowers,
>   And they crown'd her there, at the foot of the throne,
> Where, as light of love fell in quickening showers
>   About her head, they arose new-blown.

Through her poet speaker, Pfeiffer asserts that fame belongs to the temporal world and plays no part in heaven, and that a poet with no earthly identity can nevertheless join the ranks of the martyr and saint. Those who sacrifice their lives for mankind will be granted everlasting life. And finally the narrator sees the woman poet crowned with 'Song' in front of the heavenly host (p. 48):

Was it breath of perfume or breath of sound
That thrill'd through the roses sweet and strong?
I know but this: that I saw her crown'd
In the eye of heaven; and crown'd with Song.

Through her visionary narrator in 'The Crown of Song', Pfeiffer openly sets out her feminist credo: the more men try to hold women poets back, the greater will be women's reward in heaven; the more broken and dissociated women poets become when their work is derided or criticised on earth, the greater will be their reward in heaven; the more women poets inspire and assist others in the temporal world, the greater will be their reward in heaven. Unlike male poets, Pfeiffer's words imply, the woman poet may go unnamed and unrewarded on earth, but it is for this very reason that God and his Angels particularly recognise and value her sacrifices, which are on a par with those of saints and martyrs. In 'The Crown of Song' Pfeiffer promises spiritually gifted women poets an abundant reward in heaven; in the next poem I examine, Pfeiffer continues her fight for spiritual equality.

'HYMN TO THE DARK CHRISTMAS OF 1874' (1876)

In *Christina Rossetti: Faith, Gender and Time* (1999), Diane D'Amico comments on Rossetti's poem 'Paradise' (1854):

> I am not arguing that Rossetti adopted the voice of the preacher, psalmist, and prophet merely to employ a voice of power the patriarchal society denied the woman poet. . . Rather, I am suggesting that her religious faith and the reading and thoughtful study of the Bible, which was an expression of that faith, played a central role in her response to the voices of her literary foremothers, specifically to the voice of the mournful woman who sees life in terms of earthly ties and affections, as so many of Hemans's speakers do, even those who speak of the 'better land'.[41]

In her 'Hymn to the Dark Christmas of 1874' Emily Pfeiffer deliberately adopts the patriarchal voice of the preacher and prophet – but not to respond to mournful female voices of the past. Instead she warns those who still believe in 'Paradise' to look to the future – to stand up and be counted while there is still time.

'Hymn to the Dark Christmas of 1874' differs from 'The Crown of Song' in almost every way.[42] In contrast to the lyricism of 'The Crown of Song', the metre of 'Dark Christmas' is laboured and elegiac in mood; whereas 'The Crown of Song' is straightforward, 'Dark Christmas' is obscure of meaning; whereas 'The Crown of Song' is expressive, 'Dark Christmas' is intense and complex. This strange lyric poem – a 'hymn' set out as a twenty-page narrative poem – was written in response to a railway accident that occurred at Shipton, near Oxford, on Christmas Eve 1874.

Accounts of the accident are provided by the national papers, including *The Times*:[43]

> A dreadful railway accident in which 31 persons were killed and upwards of 70 wounded, occurred yesterday morning on the Great Western Railway line, a few hundred yards from the village of Hampton Gay, and close to Shipton-on-Cherwell, near Oxford . . . The train was travelling at the rate of 40 miles an hour, and the impetus given to the carriages as they left the rails carried them with terrible force for a long distance until they were finally dashed to pieces in the meadows below . . . One carriage carried away one of the stone abutments of the bridges and fell in splinters into the water. The fragments of two carriages, turned wheels upwards, were literally strewn about the embankment . . .The overturned carriages, the heartrending shrieks of the injured, the dead bodies seen in all directions . . . combined to render the spectacle horrible in the extreme . . . At the earliest opportunity telegrams were dispatched to Oxford and other places for medical assistance; but here, again, there was considerable delay, and it was about an hour and a half before a doctor appeared . . .

Pfeiffer, who had close family connections with Oxfordshire and had lived in Oxford before her marriage, was clearly upset by the Shipton train crash and also by the pall of sickness and gloom overshadowing that particular Christmas Eve, as the epigraph to her poem indicates:

> Few who dwelt under it are likely to have forgotten the cloud which hung over our English world during the late Christmas of 1874, when, in addition to prevalent sickness and manifold causes of gloom, a railway accident involving loss of life under peculiar and pathetic circumstances occurred on the eve of the festival.

In the opening stanzas to 'Dark Christmas of 1874' an authoritative voice instructs Christians to sing to 'the old triumphant tune'; to 'sing and forget'; to 'sing of the manger'; to 'sing to the shepherds'; to 'sing to the Magians'; to 'sing with the star and the angels' – Pfeiffer sets out the Christmas story of hope as song. Yet these lines do not readily lend themselves to singing. It is as if for Pfeiffer the railway disaster is too terrible to warrant a less elegiac tone. Gradually, however, an unconventional subtext emerges. Play, the didactic speaker pronounces, is important for children.[44] Adults must foster the child's innate sense of mystery, the child's belief that there must be 'a meaning, the trace of some mind, / Or many; who knows' (p. 75) behind what their senses reveal about the world (p. 76):

> To the child, unlearn'd as simple, the leap into life
>   Of the infant year,
> Is a marvel as great as the fables of any 'old wife',
>   Prophet, or seer;
>
> So it welcomes the shiftiest tale if it only profess
>   To account for a part
> Of the wonder which weighs down the world, and begins
>   now to press
>   On its innocent heart.

The narrator's emphasis on the importance of the early indoctrination of children through the Christmas story suggests a fear that their innocent hearts risk being oppressed by something that is weighing down the world:

> Let him think he may catch behind Nature a shadowy Cause,
>   Tell him not all we know!
> Lest, closed in a fortress of fact and mechanical laws,
>   He should leave off to grow.

Children must be taught even 'the shiftiest tale', including the Christmas story, so that they can grow their spiritual wings before they are clipped by being taught scientific facts. Parents must not discuss controversial scientific issues until after the children have gone to bed. Only then may parents 'build up the fragments of science' and 'tell of a Universe having nor centre nor soul, / Drifting no whither, / Making and moving itself without purpose or goal – / Hither and thither' (pp. 78–9).

Only when their children are asleep should parents pretend to rejoice in the 'Fatherless Dread' of scientific progress.

Through the didactic voice of her narrator, Pfeiffer raises the spectre of a secular world and the final destruction of the Christian faith.[45] Yet it is only at the very end of 'Dark Christmas' that she gives her reason for stressing the importance of teaching small children the Christmas story. Her motivation is this: that the children who are initiated into the Christian faith through the Christmas story today will grow up to become the Christian torch-carriers and bards of tomorrow. The small child who believes in the mysteries behind the Christmas story today will become the oracle and seer of tomorrow. If we fail to inculcate our children into the Christian faith when they are very young, the Christian religion will die out altogether. Children must be taught to follow the pattern of the immanent Christ-Child who came down to earth at Christmas to bring the good news to mankind:

> Sing with the child and the bard in his measureless youth,
>   He who, caught in the throes
> Of his passion, becomes as a Delphian mouth-piece of truth,
>   Speaking more than he knows.[46]

The carol is raised on high. Forget sorrow, sin, and death – sing of birth! The closing stanzas repeat the Yule-tide message of joy. It may be night now, but the new day is breaking.

In response to Thaïs Morgan's argument that Victorian women sometimes subverted the patriarchal model of sage discourse by entering the 'masculine' world, it seems that in 'Dark Christmas' Pfeiffer not only enters this masculine world, she seldom leaves it.[47] In the first section of 'Dark Christmas', Pfeiffer's speaker confers upon herself the authority to lecture parents on how they should bring up their children. Then she further subverts the patriarchal genre of hymnody by adopting the paternalistic tones of a sermoniser, setting out her theme, repeating it and embellishing it as she goes along. In emulating the pedantic discourse of the priestly sage, however, Pfeiffer's poem seems strangely discordant, the words tumbling over each other in a strangely oppressive way. On and on, stanza after stanza, it careens, itself like a runaway train steaming along its tracks, caught up in the power of its own momentum.

The Shipton rail crash occurred when a steam locomotive (the brain-child of scientists) became a juggernaut speeding out of control.[48] Blindly charging forward, it left its tracks and hurtled over an embankment where it smashed, killing many passengers. That being so, Pfeiffer seems to be using the disaster of the Shipton train crash as an allegory for another disaster in the making – another juggernaut, another man-made machine carrying human cargo. Like the Shipton locomotive, this juggernaut is gathering momentum, blindly lurching along man-made tracks, destined to become derailed and to fall – with appalling loss of life. But where the victims of Shipton died *physical* deaths, the victims of this new juggernaut of faithlessness are doomed to die *spiritual* deaths.

In contrast to the iron and steel of 'mechanical laws', the third section of 'Dark Christmas' starts with reference to two kinds of animals: owls and moles. Yet here too the speaker adopts the lofty tones of the scientist giving the reader the benefit of his superior knowledge of natural selection.[49] Each animal is perfectly adapted to its environment – the owl for hunting, the mole for digging. The owl's wing is adapted for skimming through the trees, but not for rising high in the sky. The mole is blind, for eyes are of no use under ground.[50] Materialists who hunt for wealth like owls, and scientists who scrabble blindly in the dark like moles, live and work according to their natures. They can choose to make their work their idol or use it to serve others. Here Pfeiffer makes her key point:

> But forbear, blind prophet, to bury the brother who sees
> 'Neath your fragments of stone!

You may think that what you know is all there is to know. *You* may delight in telling others that there is no Christmas story. *You* may believe that the hunting of material wealth (the owl) or the digging up of obscure facts (the mole) is all there is to existence. But you are a blind prophet. Just because *you* cannot see what your brother can, does not give you the right to shut out *his* light. You think you can cheat the poor by replacing hope with 'want-begotten' pleasure and blind prophecies, but can you, 'blind prophets', honestly tell the survivors of the Shipton railway disaster that the Christmas story is a fantasy, that death is *death*? So Pfeiffer berates the creators of the deadly juggernaut rushing to its doom (pp. 81–4):

He who would hunt with the owl needs a down-wadded wing,
    To skim, not to rise;
He who would grub as the mole in the fir-fangled spring,
    Is but cumber'd with eyes.

Hunt the plains of Mammon, smooth owls, when the sun is at rest,
    And with velvet clutch
Seize on the prey, – there is joy in the midnight quest,
    Gain ye little or much.

Work, dark moiler, or under the earth or above,
    And the thing ye find,
How poor soever to us, will be apt to your love,
    As made to your mind . . .

Make it your idol, or set it to serve, as you please,
    Work your will with your own,
But forbear, blind prophet, to bury the brother who sees
    'Neath your fragments of stone . . .

Ye are rich, dim owls and moles, with your hunting and finding,
    And take no heed,
No thought for the poor in the harsh mill of destiny grinding,
    Who dies in his need;

Ye forget the sorrowful poor, those whose hunger and thirst
    Is still cheated by faith,
Who, weeping lost love, can believe that great love at the worst,
    Is exalted by death.

If ye were as men, human-hearted, not burrowing brains,
    Ye would hide from the face
Of the world's vast sorrow, the sum of those terrible gains,
    Which its hope would displace.

Yet exult as you may in your 'want-begotten' delight,
    Would ye coldly dare
To carry to Shipton to-day that look-out on the night,
    Which ye warrant so fair?

In 'Dark Christmas', Pfeiffer draws attention to what she sees as a potential catastrophe in the making. She emphasises the importance of telling the Christmas story to children so that the spirit of love in the form of the immanent Christ-child is firstly enjoyed as a fairy tale, then internalised as a symbol, and then believed as a spiritual truth that can be passed down through the generations. It is vital, she insists, that the head of steam built up by myopic despoilers of faith – from the worship of science and materialism – is dissipated. A new generation of Christians must be raised to break the momentum of this dread machine before it crashes into darkness taking humanity with it.

The poem's fourth section follows the long ascent of 'our' sorrow, love and loss. The higher 'we' climb the mountain of life, the greater becomes the burden, yet love always grows as it rises and, ultimately, takes wing. Pfeiffer only once, later in this section, allows the personal pronoun to take the place of the inclusive 'we' as the hymn sings out the Christmas message. Raised in consecutive stanzas, two symbols – one of love (as a serpent) and one of death (as rebirth) – are germane to my interpretation. The first symbol of love, the serpent, Pfeiffer describes as rising from dust to a loftier plane to heal our soul-sickness, to re-affirm trust and sustain faith.

Although there are several references to serpents in the Bible, but in this case Pfeiffer is referring to John 3:1–21, where Jesus converses with the Pharisee, Nicodemus, about rebirth. Nicodemus wonders how a man can be reborn when he is old. Jesus explains that he is referring to spiritual, not physical, rebirth, and then says: 'And as Moses lifted up the serpent in the wilderness, even so must the Son of man be lifted up' (John 3:14). Jesus is referring to Numbers 21:5–9, where God sent serpents to punish the Israelites for loss of faith on their journey through the wilderness. Moses made a brass serpent and set it up high on a pole, to heal what Pfeiffer calls 'soul-sickness' and sustain faith (p. 87):

> Thus love which of old as a serpent was fed on the dust,
>   To a loftier plane
> Uplifted, shall heal our soul-sickness, build higher our trust,
>   Our new being sustain.[51]

Taking this subject further in her subsequent stanza, Pfeiffer suggests that even if the Christmas story of Jesus' birth ceases to be a symbol to mankind, it will always be there. It cannot die. Just as Jesus died and was reborn, so even if the celebration of Christ's birth dies, it will be reborn. The story will live on in perpetuity because it is immortal:

> Spread the cerements over the symbol of Jesus' birth,
>   As over a corse,
> Still the soul of the symbol, immortal, will walk the earth
>   Without hindrance or loss.

Spirit is divine – it can even pass through stone. But can we really say that no loss is incurred when the spirit is 'unhoused', when the 'bodiless Word' wanders the earth forlorn? These questions are so important to Pfeiffer that she momentarily jettisons her formal discourse in order to answer her question herself (p. 88):

> I know not, but know: when a world is baptised into youth,
>   Pass'd through fire or gore,
> A 'body' is always 'prepared', and the spirit of truth
>   Made incarnate once more.

The Christian story may seem forgotten today, Pfeiffer asserts, but there will be another day when the world is once more ready to receive the spirit of God's Truth made Man. For as long as the world endures, she vows, one truth will stand sure: 'We are made for the light' – and for ever love will redeem us (p. 89).

Witnessing the decline of 'Church' in favour of 'Chapel', the haemorrhage of High Anglicans to Roman Catholicism, and the rise of secularism and science, Pfeiffer must have felt that her particular segment of Protestantism was under siege. Despite her efforts to champion the Christian religion, it seems probable that H. A. Page would not have approved of 'Hymn to the Dark Christmas of 1874'. For Pfeiffer was definitely not sitting around embroidering emblems or singing maidenly songs, but rather she was out there with the knights 'doing battle with the enemy on his own ground, investigating the scientific bulwarks, and counter-working underground'. Although elegiac, and different in tone and character from the 'conventional' mode of poets such as Dora Greenwell and Frances Havergal – and even the 'open air' Protestant hymnody of A. L. Waring – 'Dark Christmas' is a profoundly religious poem. Setting out her own feminist agenda, Pfeiffer adopts sage discourse and enters the lists of the masculine world to fight for her faith.

The works so far discussed in this chapter show Pfeiffer, a fearless champion of women's emancipation, expressing her religious views in a short poem, a long narrative poem, and an allegory for loss of faith – all within the lyric genre. I shall now consider, within the same lyric genre, two sonnets that show the ways Pfeiffer exploited the form in support of her cause. Using the sonnet form (for which she was best known in her day), Pfeiffer marries what she sees as the moral and religious superiority of Christian women to the evolutionary concept of adaptation, change, and progress. By presenting women as having unique potential for physical and spiritual transformation through natural selection, Pfeiffer exploits Charles Darwin's evolutionary theories in order to elevate women's temporal and spiritual status. Before analysing these two sonnets, however, I first define the Petrarchan sonnet through Pfeiffer's own eyes.

In her publication entitled *Sonnets and Songs* (1880) Pfeiffer, well aware of the place of women within the sonnet tradition, wittily – and with irony – parodies courtly love in a two-sonnet sequence which might stand for a formal definition.[52] In the sestet of the first of these, 'Fallen from Grace', and in extracts from the second sonnet, 'Under the Rose', it becomes apparent that the deferred object of desire is a rose that has fallen from 'my lady's breast':

> I stoop to lift thee, and I turn aside,
> I dare not touch thee with a furtive hand,
> I dare not keep thee wanting her command,
> Nor bow before the holy thing I hide!
> But here I wait and watch, here take my stand,
> None else shall seize a joy to me denied.

In the second sonnet, Pfeiffer builds on this 'furtive' theme:

> Die, half-blown rose, upon a grateful heart,
> Whose life is quickened by thy ebbing breath . . .
> I do bestow thee where no eye may come,
> I take thee to my heart, for thou art dumb,
> And canst not mock my madness, or my moan.

These words sum up the role of 'my lady' in courtly sonnets – the possessed object of passion, the secret and silent mirror reflecting back to the lover his own image in idealised form. The lover has no interest in the personified object of his passion – in fact, the rose's death actually 'quickens' his passion. In essence, Pfeiffer makes the point that the process of fetishising women as the objects of masculine desire involves, as Elisabeth Bronfen comments, 'a metaphorical "killing" of the woman [and the process of] replacing body with sign negates her presence . . . invoking her death before its actual occurrence'.[53]

Thus in the Petrarchan sonnet the male lover worships his idealised and unobtainable love-object from afar and yet the underlying assumption of the sonnet form generally rules, as Warwick Slinn observes, that 'while self-sacrificing purity was expected of women, the ideological and scriptural authority of masculine redemption and creation was not'.[54] Thus Victorian women poets faced difficulty in positioning themselves within a tradition that silenced and disempowered them. T. D. Olverson makes the point, however, that 'in the nineteenth century, some of the greatest proponents of the sonnet were women writers'.[55] At the head of this group, alongside Michael Field and Christina Rossetti, Olverson includes Elizabeth Barrett Browning who, as Joseph Phelan recounts, determined 'to recover or rather create a distinctively female tradition' when she published her sonnet-sequence *Sonnets from the Portuguese* (1850).[56] This publication represents a turning point in Victorian poetry.

In her chapter 'Canonization through Dispossession: Elizabeth Barrett Browning and the "Pythian Shriek"', Tricia Lootens describes the poet's commitment to the issue of 'feminine canonicity':

> Surely few women poets can have been more deeply and explicitly concerned with issues of feminine canonicity than Elizabeth Barrett Browning – or more challenging, during their lifetimes, as subjects for critical attempts at stabilizing the poet-heroine's role. E.B.B. worked actively to enter and shape that role . . . [Her] career could be read as one long succession of attempts to accommodate – and to alter – the shape of feminine literary canonicity.[57]

And yet, as Lootens comments, Barrett Browning's sonnet-sequence, *Sonnets from the Portuguese*, nearly lost its canonical status in the years following its popular reception: 'Like their author, they have come close to being simultaneously canonized and lost'.[58] Accounting for this strange phenomenon, Lootens suggests that Sonnet 43 ('How do I love thee? Let me count the ways') entered the popular culture in a way that obscured the sacred nature of the sonnet-sequence as a whole. Referring to a strange heaviness in parts of the work, Lootens adds: 'Although the *Sonnets* have long defined E.B.B.'s fame, they themselves have not been defined as suitable objects for critical attention'.[59]

After her publication of *Sonnets*, where she reverses the tradition of the amatory sonnet by expressing romantic desire in a woman's voice,

Barrett Browning's 'saintly' reputation was further critically devalued after the appearance of later, still more contentious works such as *Aurora Leigh* (1856). 'Thus', comments Lootens, 'by the time Barrett Browning died, her significance as a poet and a national, cultural, and political figure was deeply controversial'.[60] Yet *Sonnets from the Portuguese* was hugely influential to sonneteers writing later in the nineteenth century; and, as Phelan points out, when Barrett Browning 'domesticated' the amatory sonnet tradition by overlaying it with Victorian morality, she was breaking new ground:

> This superimposition of nineteenth-century life and morals onto the early Renaissance template of the amatory sonnet sequence provided Barrett's successor . . . with a powerful and resonant model for the exploration of contemporary beliefs and illusions about love and marriage.[61]

Dante Gabriel Rossetti (1828–82) can be considered Barrett Browning's successor because he too 'domesticated' the amatory sonnet by superimposing nineteenth-century moral values upon the physical and spiritual dynamics of married love.[62] Responding to her brother's amatory sonnet-sequence *The House of Life* (1870, 1881), Christina Rossetti (1830–94) subsequently wrote *Monna Innominata: A Sonnet of Sonnets* (1881), a sonnet-sequence steeped in biblical and scriptural references. Although Christina Rossetti acknowledges her debt to Barrett Browning, referring to the 'Portuguese Sonnets' in her introduction, *Monna Innominata* lacks a corporeal dimension.

All three sonnet-sequences (Elizabeth Barrett Browning's *Sonnets from the Portuguese*, Dante Gabriel Rossetti's *The House of Life*, and Christina Rossetti's *Monna Innominata*) are, essentially, religious works. Yet it seems that Christina Rossetti's sonnet-sequence, *Monna Innominata*, has been critically regarded as somehow *more* religious than the sonnet-sequences of Barrett Browning and Dante Gabriel Rossetti – as if physical love, albeit within the holy state of matrimony, was somehow incompatible with spiritual purity. In addition, Christina Rossetti's close conformity to the dominant devotional literary mode of her day may have added to the general view that *Monna Innominata* was a work of greater spirituality. Phelan appears to endorse this opinion when he quotes G. B. Tennyson as saying that Christina Rossetti was regarded as 'the true inheritor of the Tractarian devotional mode in poetry':

> In [Christina Rossetti's] work the well-established trad
> ition of seeing the sonnet as a privileged vehicle for
> autobiographical utterance meets the Tractarian doctrine of
> reserve to produce poetry which is both deeply personal and
> carefully depersonalised.[63]

G. B. Tennyson and Joseph Phelan see Christina Rossetti as the true inheritor of the Tractarian devotional mode in poetry, a mode that tended to rank the 'depersonalised' doctrine of reserve higher than the 'autobiographical' outpourings of the traditional amatory sonnet. Perhaps the amatory sonnet-sequences of Elizabeth Barrett Browning and Dante Gabriel Rossetti lost canonicity because they clashed with the 'depersonalised' mode that had come to represent devotional poetry in the nineteenth century. For similar reasons, I suggest, Emily Pfeiffer's reputation may not have been served by her inclusion of scientific and emancipationist material in her religious sonnets.

As a central Anglican, Pfeiffer's religious sonnets failed to conform to the prevailing criteria for what, until recently, constituted the religious sonnet. Only now is she coming to be recognised as a religious poet of exceptional vision and perspicacity. Today, in the twenty-first century, definitions that confined the canon of women's religious poetry to the Tractarian literary mode are dissolving, for it is now increasingly understood that, for many Victorians, emotive topics such as scientific discovery and women's emancipation had religious implications of the utmost importance. Today, more flexible definitions provide greater opportunities for Pfeiffer's religious works to regain the recognition and acclaim they deserve. As Mark Knight and Emma Mason write in their introduction to *Nineteenth-Century Religion and Literature* (2006):

> Theological debate was almost inseparable from philoso
> phical, scientific, medical, historical and political thought
> in the eighteenth and nineteenth centuries. To insist on
> rigid boundaries between the sacred and secular . . . is to
> demarcate religious space in a narrow and misleading man
> ner . . . Tensions between religion and other cultural forces
> are evident throughout the nineteenth century, as between
> different religious belief systems: to ignore this and argue for

an all-purpose definition of religion risks homogenizing and caricaturing beliefs.[64]

Aware of the importance of science and theological debate, and the changing status of women within that debate, Emily Pfeiffer saw no dividing line between the sacred and secular in terms of religious expression. In this regard, as Frank James suggests, the assimilation of scientific discoveries into Christian precepts was not a particular problem for Victorians until the 1870s when 'some scientific figures sought to develop the idea that there had always existed a "conflict" between science and religion, going back to the Galileo affair if not before'.[65] Referring to John William Draper's *History of the Conflict between Religion and Science* (1874), James observes that in the same year the Irish physicist John Tyndall asserted that science would 'wrest from theology, the entire domain of cosmological theory'.[66] And yet, as he goes on to note, Michael Faraday, a devout Christian, believed 'that God had written the laws of nature into the universe at the time of the Creation, in such a way that they could be discovered'.[67] Even G. H. Lewes (1817–78) reluctantly acknowledged that theology and science could co-exist. Writing in *Fortnightly Review*, Lewes commented:

> We have too many conspicuous examples of men eminent in Science and sincere in their theological professions, not to admit that the mind can follow two Logics, and can accept both the natural and the supernatural explanations. Whether the mind ought to do so, is another question.[68]

Certainly, as far as Pfeiffer was concerned, the publication of Charles Darwin's *The Origin of Species by Means of Natural Selection* (1858) and *The Descent of Man and Selection in Relation to Sex* (1871) presented no serious problems to her as a Christian, as her 1871 correspondence with Darwin regarding sexual selection shows.[69] A. N. Wilson even suggests that some Victorians thought Darwin's theory to be 'infinitely more Christian than the theory of special creation because it . . . implies the omnipresence of [God's] creative power'.[70] One such Victorian who, according to Gillian Beer, was able to assimilate Darwin's theories of natural selection and evolution into his Christian belief system was the Reverend Charles Kingsley (1819–75).

Beer writes:

> Kingsley, seeking for a way of preserving religious meaning
> in a world saturated with cruelty and beauty, found it through
> the idea of transformation implicit in and newly authenticated
> by evolutionary theory . . . His involvement with Darwin's
> theories in their first reception created the disturbance
> out of which *The Water Babies* came with extraordinary
> spontaneity.[71]

Notions of transformation, or metamorphosis, captured the imagination of late-Victorians who endeavoured to integrate new scientific theories into a Christian framework. Beer, stating that 'many Victorians were fascinated by transformation and the limits of metamorphosis', draws attention to Margaret Gatty's story about a caterpillar that cannot believe that it will one day become a butterfly.[72] The deployment of metamorphosis as a metaphor for spiritual evolution is the subject of Pfeiffer's sonnet, 'The Chrysalis' (1876).[73]

'THE CHRYSALIS' (1876)

The form of 'The Chrysalis' is structured around the so-called 'sonnet-wave', a contemporary melodic convention which, according to Thomas Hall Caine, 'embraces the flow and ebb of thought or sentiment, and flow and ebb of music'.[74] In the Preface to his anthology, Hall Caine observes: 'It was Mr. [Theodore] Watts who first explained [the] law that is manifested in the inflowing wave solidly gathering into curving volume, culminating in one great pause, and then sweeping out again from the shore'.[75] Although Pfeiffer omits the Petrarchan 'pause' between the 'in-flowing' octave and the 'out-flowing' sestet of 'The Chrysalis', she clearly uses 'sonnet-wave' not only as a formal structure but also as a descriptive metaphor.[76] Thus Pfeiffer's sonnet operates as a formal convention to time and also as a metaphor for time, change, and progress. The octave describes the building wave – both formally and metaphorically:

> When gathering shells cast upwards by the waves
> Of Progress, they who note its ebb and flow,
>   Its flux and re-flux, surely come to know
> That the sea-level rises; that dark caves
> Of ignorance are flooded, and foul graves
>   Of sin are cleansed; albeit the work is slow;

> Till, seeing great from less for ever grow,
> Law comes to mean for them the Love that saves!

The shells 'cast upwards' by 'the waves of Progress' form part of an inevitable evolutionary process of flux and re-flux, flow and ebb – Pfeiffer's tidal imagery emulating this permanent rhythm as the waves continuously fall back to their previous state. Yet, in the first quatrain, the speaker states that shell gatherers, who 'note' the flow and ebb of tides, know that flux is stronger than re-flux. And they know this, not through superstition or belief, but through observation. Scientific method proves that sea-levels always rise. And just as, in Hall Caine's words, the 'inflowing wave solidly gather[s] into curving volume' – as the sonnet-wave reaches its crescendo near the end of the octave – so the metaphorical flood-waves also reach their peak – the two 'fluxes' of Progress (formal and metaphorical) converge, both cleansing the caves of ignorance and purging graves of sin.

Pfeiffer's emphatically rhymed metaphors of 'dark caves' and 'foul graves' are of particular interest in this context. Caves are womb-like enclosures, secret and sacred, symbolising the plight of Victorian mothers whose wombs are their destinies. Yet Pfeiffer's speaker knows that the time will come when the dark caves of ignorance will be flooded and washed clean. One day women will be set free from the chains that hold them captive because of their procreative role. True to the science of evolutionary progress from simple to complex forms so, over time, the 'graves' of women made 'foul' by patriarchal Law will be cleansed. Then shall scientists (shell-gatherers) come to understand that it is matriarchal 'Love that saves'.

In the sestet, the speaker 'lean[s] down the ages', as if from a higher vantage-point, listening:

> And leaning down the ages, my dull ear,
>   Catching their slow-ascending harmonies,
> I am uplift of them, and borne more near,
>   I feel within my flesh – laid pupa-wise –
> A soul of worship, tho' of vision dim,
> Which links me with wing-folded cherubim.

Conforming to the convention of sonnet-wave, the tide is ebbing and the progress made by the cleansing flow of the previous tide seems lost. Yet during this period of re-flux, the speaker nevertheless describes herself as 'uplift' – literally 'elated' – by these 'slow-ascending harmonies' – harmonies which intimate to her soul that the overall trend is upward. She is aware that although the feminine soul is still at an early stage of evolution, buffeted by the ebbs and flows of Progress like shells on the seashore, it is nevertheless undergoing a profound transformation. Deep within her 'flesh' the speaker knows that, over time, her soul will evolve into a more perfect form and that this form will bring her closer to 'wing-folded cherubim'.

Although Pfeiffer conforms to the male-inscribed letter of the sonnet form, she does not conform to the male-inscribed spirit of the sonnet tradition. Transforming the law (the patriarchal Letter) of sonnet-wave into a metaphor for the evolution of 'the Love that saves' (the matriarchal spirit of worship), Pfeiffer's sonnet spells out the evolutionary potential of the feminine soul. More than a decade later, in the Preface to *Flowers of the Night* (1889), published shortly before her death, Pfeiffer was to confirm her position on spiritual transformation with these words: 'In the course of evolution a track which connects the life of Time with the life Eternal is ever widening.'

THE COMING DAY (1880)

Published four years after 'The Chrysalis', Pfeiffer's sonnet 'The Coming Day' (1880) shows greater confidence in women's spiritual outcome:[77]

> In dream I saw a vision of the world
>   Caught in mid-space, a heavy-laden ship
>   Panting and bounding in a squall's fierce grip,
> Her hatches battened and her canvas furled,
> Reeling on slippery crests of waves which swirled
>   From under her, and let her blindly dip
>   Into their clamorous caves beneath the whip
> Of winds which on her hope defiance hurled.
>
> But lo, when that swift squall had swept ahead,
>   I marvelled at the way the ship had won,
> How, straight in doubt and darkness she had sped,
>   Borne by the storm-winged messenger of One
> Unnameable; and last, I saw her spread
>   All sail, and signal back the rising sun.

Pfeiffer uses the metaphor of a ship in a storm to represent the world ploughing forward in time and space, its destiny unknown. The ship is female, and Pfeiffer uses nautical imagery to describe her battening down her hatches, adapting to the adverse environmental conditions. With sails tightly furled, like a tightly corseted woman, she pants and reels and dips blindly into 'clamorous caves' under the 'whip of winds' from above. Caught between the dark depths below her (the drag of her procreative role) and the whipping winds above her (patriarchal domination), her hopes are defied. Yet, after the storm, the speaker marvels at the straight course she has steered, borne by a storm-winged Angel sent from God. The ship speeds on in full sail, signalling the rising sun. The Son is risen; the Christian world is safe; the Christian world is *woman*.

Notes

1. Isobel Armstrong, *Victorian Poetry: Poetry, Poetics and Politics* (London: Routledge, 1993), pp. 332–3.

2. Emily Pfeiffer, 'Gerard's Monument', in *Gerard's Monument and Other Poems* (London: C. Kegan Paul, 1873), p. 83.

3. Armstrong, op. cit., p. 333. See William Michael Rossetti, ed., *Poetical Works of Mrs. Felicia Hemans* [1873] (London: William Collins, n.d.), p. 16.

4. Ibid., p. 320.

5. *Pall Mall Gazette*, 11 February 1876. This unfavourable review pre-dates the 1880s and 1890s when Alice Meynell, Katharine Tynan Hinkson, and Rosamund Marriott Watson wrote for the paper.

6. Emily Pfeiffer, *Poems* (London: Strahan, 1876), pp. 13–14.

7. Op. cit., pp. 339–40. Armstrong writes that 'Victorian expressive theory is affective and of the emotions. It is concerned with feeling. It psychologised, subjectivised and often moralised the firm epistemological base of Romantic theory, though its warrant was in Wordsworth's spontaneous *overflow* of feeling' (p. 340).

8. Ibid., p. 342, quoting from Dora Greenwell's, *Essays* (London, 1866).

9. Emily Pfeiffer, *Valisneria, or A Midsummer Day's Dream: A Tale in Prose* (London: Longman, Brown, Green, 1857), p. 301.

10. I here define Atheism as a religion. Emanuel Swedenborg's visionary writings interested Elizabeth Barrett Browning and others. 'Hylo-idealism' was practised by Constance Naden.

11. John Keble, *Lectures on Poetry (1832–41)*, 2 vols (Oxford: Clarendon, 1912), 1, 22. The Tractarian theory of reserve is also associated with Isaac Williams (Tracts 80 and 87).

12. Lowther Clarke, *Historical Companion to Hymns Ancient & Modern*, ed. Maurice Frost (London: William Clowes, 1962), Introduction, p. 120.

13. A. A. Procter herself converted from High Anglicanism to Roman Catholicism.

14. Emma Mason, *John Keble in Context*, ed. Kirstie Blair (London: Anthem Press, 2004), p. 125.

15. G. B. Tennyson, *Victorian Devotional Poetry: Tractarian Mode* (London: Harvard University Press, 1981), p. 5.

16. H. A. Page, 'Religious Poetry and Scientific Criticism', *Contemporary Review* 12 (1869), 115–27 (p. 118). As a regular contributor to *Contemporary Review*, Pfeiffer would probably have read this article.

17. Ibid., p. 117. Page is referring to Dora Greenwell, *Carmina Crucis* (London: Bell & Daldy, 1869) and F. R. Havergal, *Ministry of Song* (London: Christian Book Society, 1862).

18. See *The Victorians: An Anthology*, ed. Valentine Cunningham (Oxford: Blackwell, 2000), p. 519.

19. H. A, Page, op. cit., 118.

20. Ibid., p. 123.

21. Ibid. Page refers to A. L. Waring, *Hymns and Meditations* (1850).

22. Ibid., pp. 126–7.

23. Ibid., p. 127.

24. Emily Pfeiffer, *Gerard's Monument and Other Poems* (London: C. Kegan Paul, 1873), p. 189. I use the first line of the poem as the title.

25. Ibid.

26. John 13:8.

27. John 13:9.

28. John 13:10.

29. Emily Pfeiffer, *Poems* (London: Strahan, 1876), pp. 40–8.

30. Elizabeth Barrett Browning, 'Human Life's Mystery' [c. 1844], *Poetical Works* (London: Henry Frowde, 1904), p. 291.

31. Karen Dieleman, 'Elizabeth Barrett Browning's Religious Poetics: Congregationalist Models of Hymnist and Preacher', *Victorian Poetry* 45 (2007), 135–57 (p. 135).

32. Ibid., p. 135, quoting Thaïs Morgan, 'Victorian Sage Discourse and the Feminine: An Introduction', in Morgan, ed., *Victorian Sages and Cultural Discourses: Renegotiating Gender and Power* (New Brunswick: Rutgers University Press, 1990), p. 6.

33. Ibid., p. 136.

34. Ibid.

35. Ibid., p. 137.

36. Ibid., p. 138.

37. The 'apostolic' authority of priests in the Church of England is believed to derive from the apostles who were imbued with the Holy Spirit, while Congregationalist priests are ordinary, albeit learned, individuals trained to preach and give guidance to their fellows.

38. Emily Pfeiffer, op. cit., p. 298.

39. Dieleman, op. cit., p. 136.

40. Thomas Carlyle, *Heroes, Hero-Worship and the Heroic in History* (London: George Routledge, 1840), pp. 108–9.

41. Diane D'Amico, *Christina Rossetti: Faith, Gender and Time* (Baton Rouge: Louisiana State University Press, 1999), p. 30.

42. Emily Pfeiffer, *Poems*, op. cit., pp. 70–90. (Henceforth 'Dark Christmas'.)

43. *The Times*, 25 December, 1874, p. 3.

44. A German speaker, Pfeiffer may have been familiar with the ideas of Friedrich Froebel (1782–1852) on the importance of play for young children.

45. Emily Pfeiffer, a member of the Established Church, was witnessing the decline of church congregations. Nonconformism and High Church denominations, however, were flourishing despite the rise in science and secularism.

46. Emily Pfeiffer, *Poems*, op. cit., p. 90.

47. Dieleman, op. cit., p. 135, quoting Morgan, op. cit., p. 6.

48. Pfeiffer may be referring to agnostic scientists such as Herbert Spencer (1820–1903) who had at one time been a railway engineer.

49. In 1871, Pfeiffer corresponded with Charles Darwin on the subject of sexual selection in the Argus pheasant. She appears to have been knowledgeable on the subject.

50. Biblical references to these animals are few. In Leviticus 11:16–17 and Psalms 102:6, the owl is referred to as an 'unclean' animal whose flesh must not be eaten. Biblical references to moles are less forthcoming, depending on the translation, but in *A Priest in the Temple*, George Herbert's poem 'Grace' (1633) describes how 'Death is still working like a mole, / And digs my grave at each remove'.

51. A snake coiled around a pole, or caduceus, is also the symbol of healing adopted by the medical profession, though this derives equally from classical antiquity.

52. Emily Pfeiffer, *Sonnets and Songs* (London: C. Kegan Paul, 1880), pp. 40–1.

53. Elisabeth Bronfen, *Over Her Dead Body: Death, Femininity and the Aesthetic* (Manchester: Manchester University Press, 1992), p. 119.

54. Warwick Slinn, 'Poetry', in *A Companion to Victorian Literature and Culture*, ed. Herbert F. Tucker (Oxford: Blackwell, 2002), p. 317.

55. T. D. Olverson, *Women Writers and the Dark Side of Late-Victorian Hellenism* (Basingstoke, Hampshire: Palgrave Macmillan, 2010), pp. 86–7.

56. Joseph Phelan, *The Nineteenth-Century Sonnet* (Basingstoke, Hampshire: Palgrave Macmillan, 2005), p. 55

57. Tricia Lootens, *Lost Saints: Silence, Gender and Victorian Literary Canonization* (London: University Press of Virginia, 1996), p. 121.

58. Ibid., p. 116.

59. Ibid.

60. Ibid., p. 128.

61. Phelan, op. cit., p. 59.

62. George Meredith, a friend of Dante Gabriel Rossetti, was another successor to *Sonnets from the Portuguese*. Meredith's sonnet-sequence *Modern Love* (1862) reflects upon the domestic difficulties that may have contributed to his wife's death.

63. Phelan, op. cit., p. 94, initially quoting G. B. Tennyson.

64. Mark Knight and Emma Mason, *Nineteenth-Century Religion and Literature: Introduction* (Oxford: Oxford University Press, 2006), p. 3.

65. Frank James, 'Science & Religion', *London Library Magazine* 12 (2011), 16–18 (p. 16).

66. Ibid.

67. Ibid.

68. G. H. Lewes, 'On the Dread and Dislike of Science', *Fortnightly Review* 23 (1878), 318.

69. Emily Pfeiffer, *Correspondence of Charles Darwin* (Darwin Correspondence Project, University of Cambridge, 2007), Letters 7411 and 7719f, vol. 19).

70. A. N. Wilson, *God's Funeral* (London: John Murray, 1999), p. 191.

71. Gillian Beer, *Darwin's Plots, Evolutionary Narratives in Darwin, George Eliot and Nineteenth-Century Fiction*, 2nd edn (Cambridge: Cambridge University Press, 2000), p. 127.

72. Ibid., p. 131.

73. Kathleen Hickok, '"Intimate Egoism": Reading and Evaluating Noncanonical Poetry by Women', *Victorian Poetry* 33 (1995), 13–30 (pp. 17–19). In her interpretation of 'The Chrysalis', Hickok refers to the religious element in Pfeiffer's words. Hickok interprets 'That dark caves / Of ignorance are flooded' as meaning 'that ignorance will inevitably be flooded with truth, and, in a baptismal image, that sin will inevitably (and consequently) be cleansed'. Hickok adds: 'Thus Pfeiffer claims for herself a sanctified role as poet-prophet: her mission is to reconcile and to inspire'.

74. Thomas H. Hall Caine, ed., *Sonnets of Three Centuries: Selection* (London: Elliot Stock, 1882), p. 22.

75. Ibid.

76. Catherine Brennan, 'Emily Jane Pfeiffer and the dilemma of progress', *Angers, Fantasies and Ghostly Fears: Nineteenth-century Women from Wales and English-language Poetry* (Cardiff: University of Wales Press, 2003), p. 143. From a postcolonial perspective, Brennan sees 'The Chrysalis' as a sonnet relating to 'the forces of economic, political and social amelioration' in mid-Victorian Britain.

77. Emily Pfeiffer, *Sonnets and Songs* (London: C. Kegan Paul, 1880), p. 96. After the fire at C. Kegan Paul, Trench & Co. in 1882, the book's title was revised as *Sonnets* (London: Field & Tuer, 1886).

CHAPTER TWO

Changing Christian Images

I N T H I S C H A P T E R I will investigate three poems that show Emily Pfeiffer attempting to reconcile her Christian faith with her emancipationist values. Although by the late 1870s her poetry is starting to reflect the mismatch between her faith and her feminism (exacerbated by the rapid growth of the women's movement in that decade), she nevertheless takes advantage of themes and poetic techniques deployed by women writing earlier in the century.

In the first poem under discussion, 'A Song of Winter' (1879), Pfeiffer reflects the influence of a poem called 'Lessons from the Gorse', which was published by Elizabeth Barrett Browning in 1841.[1] In the second, her ballad 'Madonna Dūnya' (1879), Pfeiffer's description of an icon of the Virgin Mary brings to mind Adelaide Procter's description of the White Maiden in 'A Tomb in Ghent' (1855).[2] In the third, an epic romance entitled 'From Out of the Night' (1882), Pfeiffer conveys the drama of premonition with great effect – as had Christina Rossetti in her poem 'My Dream' (1855), where an avenging ghost flies over the Euphrates casting its shadow over the sand.[3] Building on the poetic talents of these and other contemporaries, Pfeiffer leaves her own original and inimitable imprint on three topics important to women at that time: women and Mother Nature; women and the Virgin Mother; and Fallen Women.

WOMEN AND MOTHER NATURE: 'A SONG OF WINTER' (1879)[4]

In the late 1870s Emily Pfeiffer, aware of the male-inscribed view of women as being closer than men to the natural world because of their procreative role, inverted this image to present women as being closer than men to Jesus precisely because of their procreative role. Scriptural doctrine promulgated notions that linked sex and procreation to sin and death in ways that demeaned and marginalised women within the Established Church. Victorian girls inculcated into the Christian faith unconsciously absorbed and internalised negative attitudes relating to their reproductive functions. In her short lyric poem, an elegy entitled 'A Song of Winter' (1879), however, Pfeiffer subverts this misogyny by alluding to the 'stigma' (the female sexual apparatus) of a plant species that blooms throughout the winter. Here it seems likely that Pfeiffer intended her formal elegy to hold particular significance for women who, denied the opportunity to study science, were often taught botany instead. For these women, the botanical term 'stigma' would have had special meaning.

Constructing her elegy around the word 'stigma', Pfeiffer clearly intends her speaker to be identified as female. Thus, addressing the flower of the gorse directly, she acknowledges her love for its blossoms which brighten wintry days when other flowers are dead. In the second stanza of eight, she reveals her primary interest – that gorse is 'undying':

> Flower of the gorse, the rose is dead,
>   Thou art undying, O be mine!
> Be mine with all thy thorns, and prest
> Close on a heart that asks not rest.

The speaker then begs the gorse flower, emblematic of everlasting life, to be hers – thorns and all:

> I pluck thee and thy stigma set
>   Upon my breast and on my brow,
> Blow, buds, and plenish so my wreath
> That none may know the wounds beneath.

The speaker plucks the gorse blossom and sets its 'stigma' on her breast and brow, the blossoms forming a wreath to hide her wounds. In this way, Pfeiffer verbally links the 'stigma' of the gorse flower to the 'stigmata', or wounds, associated with woman's procreative physiology. Having made this connection, Pfeiffer is then able to link these senses of the word directly to the 'stigmata' of the crucified Jesus. This connection is supported by a stanza in which the speaker describes the golden gorse shining out like a beacon on the hill as winter approaches:

> And yet thy lamp upon the hill
> Feeds on the autumn's dying sigh,
> And from thy midst comes murmuring
> A music sweeter than in spring.

As the gorse flower survives winter, so Jesus, crucified on a hill called Golgotha, survives death. Gorse and Jesus are undying, and because the female speaker shares their stigmata she knows that she too is undying. In this elegy, Pfeiffer situates women right alongside Jesus' crucifixion and resurrection. Women, because of their Christ-like suffering, will survive death.

WOMEN AND THE VIRGIN MOTHER: 'MADONNA DŪNYA' (1879)

From today's perspective, looking back to the maltreatment of women during the Victorian period – a maltreatment supported not only by British law but also by the Established Church – it is hard to imagine what life must have been like, especially for married women. That wives were still subject to patriarchy in every area of their lives is endorsed by the words of John Stuart Mill in *The Subjection of Women* (1869). Harriet Taylor (1807–58) was the inspiration for, if not the author of, these words:

> The wife is the actual bondservant of her husband: no less so . . . than slaves . . . She vows a lifelong obedience to him at the altar, and is held to it all through her life by law . . . If she leaves her husband, she can take nothing with her, neither her children nor anything which is rightfully her own. If he chooses, he can compel her to return, by law, or by physical force; or he may content himself with seizing for his own use anything which she may earn, or which may be given to her by her relations.[5]

In terms of religion, one of the difficulties faced by women who wanted to construct more gynocentric symbols and images was the fact that to do so involved betraying, to some extent, the male-inscribed biblical tenets of the Christian faith. This proved to be a stumbling block for many of Pfeiffer's religious contemporaries – poets who, because their faith demanded close conformity to High Anglican and Roman Catholic dogmatism, found themselves up against a doctrinal brick wall. As a middle-of-the-road Protestant, however, Pfeiffer was better placed to operate both inside and outside patriarchal orthodoxy than her female contemporaries, and because of this she may usefully be compared with Anna Jameson (1794–1860), the central Anglican author of *Legends of the Madonna* (1852). Regarding Jameson's treatment of the Virgin Mother, Kimberly VanEsveld Adams writes:

> Jameson's feminist Mariology qualifies the assumption of many feminist scholars in the fields of religion, history, and literature . . . that the Virgin Mary is so closely linked to the misogynistic practices and oppressive politics of the patriarchal Church and male-dominated societies that historically she has served only as a distorted and repressive ideal for women. Jameson is able to see the Madonna in new ways because of her Protestantism and her profession. This Victorian writer balances her reverence for what previous generations considered holy and precious with a Protestant's freedom to appropriate or reject the religious past. And like Grimké and [Elizabeth Cady] Stanton she has a Protestant's confidence that she may interpret the ancient legends, liturgies, and sacred images for herself, and find what she calls their living spirit. Jameson reveals herself as a worshipper of the feminine divine . . . and she brings the Virgin Mother down to earth, using this powerful image to advance the causes of progressive religion and sexual equality.[6]

Adams makes several important points here. Like the scholarship she cites, she is aware that the Virgin Mary is linked to misogynistic practices and serves as a 'distorted and repressive' role-model for women. Adams suggests that Jameson has a 'Protestant's freedom to appropriate or reject the religious past', feeling free, she argues, to interpret ancient legends, images, and liturgies herself in order to find 'their living spirit'. Jameson worships the feminine divine, yet uses images of the 'Virgin Mother' to advance the causes of 'progressive religion and sexual equality'.

Jameson's reverence for the Virgin Mother is coupled with a desire to bring her down to earth – to eliminate what she describes as 'the relics of many an ancient faith'.[7] In *Legends of the Madonna*, for example,

Jameson draws attention to the amalgamation of the Madonna with Diana of Ephesus (the pagan goddess of both chastity and fertility) in early art forms:

> [The Madonna] became . . . the impersonation of motherhood . . . and at the same time, by virtue of her perpetual virginity, the patroness of single and ascetic life – the example and the excuse for many of the wildest of the early monkish theories . . . Christ, as they assure us, was born of a woman only, and had no earthly father . . . Therefore we are to suppose that, for the exaltation of the male sex, Christ appeared on earth as a man; and, for the consolation of womankind, he was born of a woman only . . . But also with Christianity came the want of a new type of womanly perfection, combining all the attributes of the ancient female divinities with others altogether new. Christ, as the model-man, united the virtues of the two sexes, till the idea that there are essentially masculine and feminine virtues intruded itself on the higher Christian conception, and seems to have necessitated the female type.[8]

The Fathers of the Church, men such as St Justin the Martyr (c. 100– 165 AD) and St Irenaeus (c. 130–200 AD), had ideas about feminine virtue that 'intruded' themselves upon the Christian religion. In order to create a 'model-woman', a virtuous 'female type', Mary was elevated as the great exception among women. Uncontaminated by Eve's sin and untainted by the bodily functions normally associated with female sexuality – menstruation, pregnancy, and childbirth – Mary was raised still higher when the Church insisted that she was a virgin not only before but also after Jesus' birth. Honouring Mary with perpetual virginity was apparently not enough, for in the fifth century it was proclaimed 'that Mary's unique virgin-motherhood made her "God-bearer" . . . Symbolically [this] presented Mary not only as the mother of the human Jesus but also as the Mother of God'.[9] Under the caption 'Mary the Mother of God' in the Roman Catholic treatise *Mariology*, Joseph Pohle and Arthur Preuss use the scriptures to prove 'Mary's Divine Motherhood':

> The Bible does not employ the formal term 'Mother of God', but refers to the Blessed Virgin merely as . . .'mother of the Lord'. However, since Jesus Christ is [the] true God, all texts that refer to Mary as His mother are so many proofs of her

divine maternity . . . [In Luke 1:35] the heavenly messenger expressly [said to Mary]: 'Therefore the Holy [one] which shall be born of thee shall be called the Son of God'. Since Mary gave birth to the Son of God, she is really and truly the mother of God.[10]

In her essay 'Stabat Mater', however, Julia Kristeva draws attention to translation errors and the imposition of pagan-rooted beliefs on, and against, Church dogma:

It would seem that the 'virgin' attribute for Mary is a translation error, the translator having substituted for the Semitic term that indicates the socio-legal status of a young unmarried woman the Greek work parthenos, which on the other hand specifies a physiological and psychological condition: virginity . . . The fact remains that Western Christianity has organized that 'translation error', projected its own fantasies into it and produced one of the most powerful imaginary constructs known in the history of civilizations. The story of the virginal cult in Christianity amounts in fact to the imposition of pagan-rooted beliefs on, and often against, dogmas of the official Church . . . [The Gospels] suggest only very discreetly the immaculate conception of Christ's mother, they say nothing concerning Mary's own background and speak of her only seldom at the side of her son or during the crucifixion . . . In the rare instances when the Mother of Jesus appears in the Gospels, she is informed that filial relationship rests not with the flesh but with the name or, in other words, that any possible matrilinearism is to be repudiated and the symbolic link alone is to last.[11]

Kristeva asserts that the cult of the Virgin Mary originates from pagan-based beliefs, combined with a crucial translation error of the word *parthenos*, both of which were imposed upon the dogmatism of the Church. Marina Warner, writing of the cult surrounding Mary, also draws attention to the dearth of information about her birth, life, and death. Warner criticises the way Roman Catholic educators imposed 'nearly two thousand years of sexual chastity' on children as a result of their interpretation of what they saw as Mary's 'purity':[12]

That the mother of God should be a virgin was a matter of such importance to the men of the early Church that it overrode all other considerations . . . Sexuality represented to them the gravest danger and the fatal flaw . . . It is almost impossible to overestimate the effect that the characteristic Christian association of sex and sin and death has had on the attitudes of our civilization.[13]

The recent Tate Britain exhibition 'Art Under Attack' (2013–14) displayed some of the religious works of art disfigured by iconoclasts following the break with Rome during and after the reign of Henry Tudor. Reporting on the exhibition, the art critic Waldemar Januszczak observed that whereas iconoclasm was elsewhere presented as a destructive force, when it came to the iconoclasm of the suffragette movement represented in the same exhibition (and exemplified by the slashing of Velazquez's *Rokeby Venus* by the suffragist Mary Richardson in 1914) it is 'suddenly the only way to achieve a rightful cause'.[14] Quoting a caption at the exhibition claiming that 'For the suffragettes, the idealisation of inanimate objects while real women were treated with indifference was the real outrage',[15] Januszczak draws attention to the fact that for twentieth-century suffragists the Virgin Mother served as what Kimberly VanEsveld Adams describes as a 'repressive and distorted feminine ideal'. Emily Pfeiffer's ballad 'Madonna Dūnya', however, exploits the cult of the Virgin Mary to advance a feminist reconstruction of Christian dogma.

In 'Madonna Dūnya' (1879) – a ballad that she assures her readers is only loosely based on a Russian saga – Emily Pfeiffer exploits the concept of motherhood in order to situate a woman at the very pinnacle of heaven.[16] By superimposing images of the Virgin and Child upon those of a peasant mother and her baby, Pfeiffer presents an image of motherhood that transcends the negative role traditionally foisted upon women by the Church. Thus a human mother is spiritually elevated through the intervention of an icon of the Virgin Mother, while the icon is itself reanimated and reconnected to the spiritual power Christian iconographers denied her.

The ballad consists of sixty-eight four-line stanzas of iambic tetrameters, a measure commonly adopted by hymnists and ballad-writers. But in 'Madonna Dūnya' Pfeiffer avoids lapsing into the hymn-like 'sing-song' of 'Long Metre' by interspersing dactyls, pyrrhics, and anapaests among the iambs, thereby constructing line-lengths of eight, nine, ten, and eleven, syllables. The resulting irregularity gives the ballad pace and energy.

To obviate problems relating to the length and complexity of this work, and for readers unfamiliar with it, I supply below a brief précis of the narrative before selecting four motifs for discussion.

> Dūnya, a peasant woman, crosses the snow-laden Russian steppes in search of work. Eventually she reaches the house of Grunya, the Bolshūka (or peasant matriarch). Dūnya enters the house and kneels before an icon of the Virgin Mary and Child. Dūnya is also carrying her baby boy under her sheepskin. Although there is no work to be had, Dūnya finally persuades Grunya to let her work in the fields with her baby. But the earth is sick and animals are dying, and in the summer heat Dūnya contracts the Black Death. Desperate not to contaminate her son, Dūnya leaves him at a wayside cross, and crawls away to die on her own. The boy is brought to the Bolshūka's house, where he cries for his mother all day, but is strangely happy and contented at night. Every night the women of the household hear the boy laughing, and every morning they notice he has milk on his lips. So they spy on the child one night and witness a miracle: a woman is breast-feeding the child. At first they think the icon of the Virgin Mary is feeding the baby, but then they realise that it is Dūnya, wearing the Madonna's golden stole. Dūnya's ghost sees them watching her, and reluctantly leaves. Soon afterwards, the baby dies. Grunya and the other women of the house hear the sound of a horse-drawn chariot approaching and witness another miracle: Elijah has come to take the mother (in the golden stole) and child up to heaven.

In this ballad – a pseudo-saga set far enough away both in time and space to protect its author from unfavourable criticism – Pfeiffer's description of Dūnya crossing the barren steppe is interspersed with an oppressive undercurrent of evil that bodes ill for the young woman. In the first stanza Pfeiffer identifies this evil as the earth, 'dead in her winding-sheet' (p. 59). In the fourth stanza she describes the earth as having 'the face of a corpse / With the dead-locked secret beneath its smile' – the smile performing the same function as the snow which, like a 'winding sheet', conceals the rottenness of the earth beneath it. (pp. 59–60). The earth is personified as a rotting carcass, its centre – the town – exuding the stench of death and decay (p. 67):

> So passed the days, so passed the nights;
> The sun rose early, and late went down;
> A change came over the earth's dead face,
> The smell of death rose rank from the town.

There seems to be something wrong with the earth, even though the spring arrives with its usual sweetness. The other women in the Bolshūka's house hint at some kind of debilitating condition sapping their strength (p. 68):

> And the women spake: 'We are frail and spent,
> And our men from the homestead are wandering free
> We bid you stay for your own young strength,
> And the sake of the child who is frailer than we.'

Then the animals and birds start to die and Dūnya grows increasingly aware of 'the fiend that was haunting the Don' (p. 70). Here, as throughout the ballad, Dūnya is depicted as a victim of the earth, whose evil smile conceals a 'dead-locked secret'. The earth is smiling because she knows that she is the purveyor of disease and death, and that the earth always takes back her own – dust to dust, ashes to ashes – thus motherhood means both life and death. Mothers and their sons must die, rot, and return to Mother Earth.

The second motif relates to the poetic techniques adopted by Pfeiffer to infer a two-way relationship between Dūnya and the icon (or *eikon*) of the Virgin Mother and Child.

On the subject of icons, Jane Harrison writes:

> Eikonism takes the vague, unknown, fearful thing, and tries to picture it as known, as distinct, definite – something a man can think about and understand; something that will think about and understand him . . . The vague some*thing* becomes a particular some*one* . . . they give him a life-story and provide him with human relations: eikonism generates immediate mythology. For mythology is only, like eikonism, the attempted expression of the unknown in terms of the known . . . Shaping no human form, aneikonism tells no human story, has no mythology, no human genealogy, no pseudo-history.[17]

Arriving at the house, Dūnya speeds past the Bolshūka so that she can kneel before the icon of 'the Mother of God' (p. 61). It is as if Grunya does not exist in comparison with the icon. Under her sheepskin Dūnya is sheltering her baby (p. 62):

> Fair to her greeting the Icon smiled,
>> Holding her babe to her mother's breast,
> Smiled in the flickering light of her lamp,
>> Telling of comfort, and eke of rest . . .
>
> A three-month's child in its rosy sleep,
>> A child as the Christ of the Icon fair,
> Was the load which had lain on the wanderer's heart
> And stood revealed to the woman there.

The icon of the Virgin Mother smiles at Dūnya, denoting the camaraderie of two women who share the bond of motherhood – but, of course, the whole idea of an inanimate icon smiling is an illusion (like the fairy-tale fantasy of the talking mirror in *Snow White*). Pfeiffer uses the icon's smile as a device to distort reality and make the unreal appear real, and vice versa. No mortal eye can see what Dūnya is sheltering under her sheepskin, yet the icon of the Virgin Mother smiles at Dūnya because she knows that Dūnya has a baby son – and immediately the reader visualises an entirely mutual relationship between the Virgin Mother and Dūnya. Later, the other women of Grunya's household observe that Dūnya's child is as fair as Jesus had been when he was alive. Again, Pfeiffer distorts time and space by depicting the adult, crucified Jesus as a real baby alongside Dūnya's baby 'here and now' in medieval Russia. The women could not know (other than from the man-made icon) whether or not Jesus had been fair as a child; nor could they know from Dūnya's tattered appearance and prayerful attitude whether or not she was a pilgrim (p. 65):

> When the other two women came home i'the dusk,
>> They saw, 'neath the Virgin in gold and sheen,
> A tattered pilgrim who bore a child
> As fair as the living Christ had been.

Pfeiffer manipulates her account of the two women's perception of events to draw her readers into her narrative and, as she drives home Dūnya's Madonna-like qualities, she continues to blur the distinction between illusion and reality. Then Pfeiffer goes even further into the realms of the mystery by steering Dūnya away from the usual man–woman relationship.

Did she dream of a man? 'I tell you no' (p. 66):

> I tell you no, – that not Mary's self,
> The Virgin Mother, the vestal soul,
> That of mortal passion had known no throb,
> Had a heart for her first-born son more whole.

Dūnya is not grieving for a lost lover: indeed, the baby's father is not in the picture at all. For not even the Virgin Mother, who never knew the throb of 'mortal passion', loved her Son more wholly than Dūnya loved her own baby boy. This stanza can be interpreted on two levels: that Dūnya is sexually innocent and that her love for her son is pure; or that Dūnya, like the Virgin Mary, is the recipient of the God-given gift of perpetual virginity and that her baby is the living equivalent of Jesus. Pfeiffer gently drops into her readers' minds the blasphemous possibility that a Russian peasant woman and her son are on a spiritual par with the Virgin Mother and Jesus.

Later in the poem, Pfeiffer reinforces this impression when she describes three mowers emulating the Magi by crossing themselves when they see Dūnya working in the fields, lit up in the golden haze of the setting sun (p. 69):

> One eve when behind them the sun went down,
> And his beams got tangled in Dūnya's hair,
> Three mowers looked on through the golden haze
> And they crossed themselves all unaware.

Again Pfeiffer blends the images of the two mothers into a single unit of holiness.

A third motif relates to Dūnya's struggle to find employment, reflecting the efforts of emancipationists (including Pfeiffer herself) striving to help women gain work in a male-dominated labour market.[18] Dūnya is now a mother with a baby to feed, so it is vital that she finds work. She tells Grunya that she is prepared to do any kind of labouring job as long as she and her baby are allowed to stay. In the next two stanzas Dūnya's voice takes centre-stage (pp. 64–8):

> 'I will beat your hemp, I will hew your wood,
> I will do your bidding both high and low,
> And then in the spring, if you need me not,
> On St. George's day I will rise and go;

'And you bid me stay, I will drive your plough,
   Drive or draw, if your beasts are spare;
My heart is stout as my hands are strong,
   And my face – it is nothing now too fair . . .'

So she stayed and wrought; she ploughed their ground,
   And sowed the seed in their plot of the Mîr,
Till, sweet in the shade of the flowering rye,
   She laid the flower of all the year.

The rhythmical energy of these stanzas depicts Dūnya's desperation for work and, later, her vigorous labour in the fields. Although she has by now lost her looks, her hands and heart are strong, and she can labour and drive a plough as well as any man. Dūnya uses her strength to plough and shape the earth, to sow seeds and reap the harvest – a woman cultivator of the earth, rather than the earth itself as traditionally depicted.

Emily Pfeiffer's depiction of a female peasant labourer strong enough to take on the masculine role of cultivator of the land in 'Madonna Dūnya' finds an intriguing parallel in a poem called 'La Mujer Fuerte' (1922), published several years later by the Chilean poet Gabriela Mistral (1889–1957). In 'La Mujer Fuerte' the strong mother labours in the fields sowing wheat and, in her study of this work, Margaret Bruzelius observes that '[Mistral] overlay[s] the image of the peasant woman with that of the Virgin . . . In this way the peasant woman . . . becomes sacralized by the evocation of the Virgin's attributes . . .'[19] In addition, Bruzelius comments that the woman here takes 'the traditional male role as cultivator of the earth (not the female one, which is to be the earth itself)'.[20] In like manner, Dūnya, who uses her strength to cultivate the earth, is rendered sacred by her spiritual affinity with the Virgin Mother. By the same token, however, the icon of the Virgin Mother is overlaid by the physical attributes of Dūnya, particularly with regard to Dūnya's physical power to shape and cultivate the earth as well as any man. In this context it could be argued that, as the Mother of God, the Virgin Mother preceded God and was, therefore, the original creator and cultivator of the Universe.

The final motif I want to raise concerns the miracles that occur after Dūnya succumbs to the Black Death. Grunya and the women of the house are witnesses to Dūnya's ghostly visitation (p. 75):

Then up rose Grunya and broke the jar;
The pent-up light leapt forth and clung
To the sheen of the Virgin's golden stole,
And her breast where the laughing baby hung.

The women fell on their knees in prayer,
And slowly, fearfully, from her place
The mother, stoled in jewels and gold,
On the kneeling wives turned her sorrowful face;

Not the Icon's face in its passionless peace,
But the face of the wandering Dūnya glowed
On the trembling women, with mild reproach
In the eyes which the sudden tears o'flowed.

Wearing the icon's golden stole, Dūnya has returned to feed her son. The next day the baby refuses to eat or drink because 'he had tasted the milk of paradise'. Later the child dies.

The next miracle occurs when Elijah appears in his horse-drawn chariot and takes the mother and her child up to heaven. Pfeiffer explains this part of her poem in a prefatory note, stating that 'The Russ peasant expresses the poetical notion that the storms of thunder and lightning, very frequent about St. Elijah's Day, are the result of the flash and rumbling of the prophet's fiery car and steeds' (p. 58). Using this folk-tale as a justification for the miraculous conclusion of her ballad, Pfeiffer's final stanza makes interesting biblical allusions (p. 76):

Then they saw the flash of Elijah's steeds,
And they heard the wheels of his chariot roll, –
And within was a babe in his mother's arms
Made safe for the night in her golden stole.

Elijah transports a mother and child to heaven – but which mother and child is it? The mother is wearing the golden stole that adorned the icon of the Virgin Mary, the same stole that Dūnya was wearing when, as a spirit, she returned to breast-feed her baby. The symbolism of the stole, in the context of Elijah's own death and chariot-bound journey to heaven, is described in II Kings 2:8–15:

And Elijah took his mantle, and wrapped it together, and
smote the waters, and they were divided hither and thither,
so that they two went over on dry ground . . .

Behold, there appeared a chariot of fire, and horses of
fire and . . . Elijah went up by a whirlwind into heaven . . .

And Elisha saw it, and he cried, My father, my father, the
chariot of Israel, and the horsemen thereof. And he saw him
no more . . .

And he took the mantle of Elijah that fell from him, and
smote the waters, and said, Where is the Lord God of Elijah?
and when he also had smitten the waters, they parted hither
and thither: and Elisha went over.

And when the sons of the prophets which were to view
at Jericho saw him, they said, The spirit of Elijah doth rest on
Elisha. And they . . . bowed themselves to the ground before
him.

Pfeiffer seems to be making the point that, just as Elisha attains spiritual
power from his father's mantle, so Dūnya obtains spiritual power from
the Madonna's golden stole. The passing of the stole, like Elijah's
mantle, from parent to child, suggests the symbolic transfer of spiritual
power from the Virgin Mother to Madonna Dūnya.

In 'Madonna Dūnya', Emily Pfeiffer adapts a medieval prose narrative
to camouflage the transgressive content of her ballad. She exploits the
traditional fairy-tale fantasy of an inanimate object becoming animate
in order to depict an 'eikon' of the Virgin Mother coming alive because
of the maternal bond she shares with a peasant woman and her child. In
the transformation from death to life, from inanimate to animate, and,
in the case of the Virgin Mother, from 'eikon' to 'aneikon', both women
are able to overcome their inanimate states – the Virgin as a powerless
man-made icon, and the peasant as the rotting victim of an earth-
borne disease. In this poem, Pfeiffer subverts religious convention by
apparently fusing the two mothers into a single goddess: Mother, and
Creator of the World.

FALLEN WOMEN: 'FROM OUT OF THE NIGHT' (1882)[21]

In Emily Pfeiffer's epic romance 'From Out of the Night', a young
girl addresses the River Isis in the form of a soliloquy. Ruminating
on the events leading to her downfall, her sad tale is all too familiar: a
gullible girl loses her virginity to a young man who promises marriage.

Succumbing to the oldest lie in the book, the girl ends up all alone, victim to psychological, social, and religious strictures. Then drowns herself.

Pfeiffer's treatment of this subject needs to be read within a continuum of nineteenth-century 'fallen woman' poems, an early example being Dora Greenwell's dramatic monologue 'Christina' (1851), where the fallen woman dies for her sins, but is granted a place in purgatory where, during 'soul sleep', she can be spiritually prepared for the Last Judgement.[22] Christina Rossetti's 'Goblin Market' (1862) remains the focus of critical interest. As Diane D'Amico points out, 'the goblins are not primarily interested in Laura's body. Rather, through the seduction of the body, they hope to destroy her soul'.[23] In 'A Legend of Provence' (1866), Adelaide Procter writes of a nun who runs away with a soldier. Years later, the fallen woman returns to the convent only to be greeted by her double – an unblemished, virginal, version of herself. The Virgin Mary has taken her place at the convent so that upon her return she can resume her position as if she had never been away.[24] For Elizabeth Barrett Browning, Marian Erle, the woman who is drugged and raped in *Aurora Leigh* (1856), raises social, rather than religious, issues.[25] In her dramatic monologue 'A Castaway' (1870), August Webster also breaks away from tradition by separating the 'fallen woman' motif from religion altogether, comparing prostitution with immoral, male-oriented markets.[26] And in her blank-verse 'Mary Magdalene, A Poem' (1880), Sarah Dana Greenough conflates Mary Magdalene with the prostitute who dried Jesus' feet with her hair in St Luke's gospel,[27] a subject later taken up in poems by Amy Levy ('Magdalen') and Mathilde Blind ('The Message'), in 1884 and 1891 respectively.[28]

Chronologically, Pfeiffer's 'From Out of the Night' sits between Greenough's 'Mary Magdalen, A Poem' (1880) and Amy Levy's 'Magdalen' (1884). The extent to which its content fits (if it does at all) this continuum is harder to define. A middle-of-the-road Protestant, Pfeiffer did not share many of the values that inspired these contemporaries, and even though she raises social issues – as Barrett Browning does in *Aurora Leigh* – Pfeiffer tends to link them to other, more contentious, subjects. In order to evaluate the ethical complexities of Pfeiffer's wide-ranging poem, which meanders backwards and forwards in time, I shall summarise its main areas of interest under a series of sub-headings below.

Paganism

As the young orphan stands in the dark, looking into the turgid depths of the river in which she will soon end her life, she looks back on her sad childhood. She recalls 'summerless years', 'sad seasons flown', memories of having to fight for survival in a dark world without her mother. Before her mother's death she had been loved and cared for, but since then she has been 'shadow-crossed' and all alone in the world. The young girl addresses the river (p. 12):

> And I had seen summerless years with the sad seasons flown,
>> Fatherless, motherless, having to fight for my share,
> A poor place in the shadow-crossed world which had not been my own
>> When the heart of a mother had held me from the shadow of care.

Despite her grinding poverty, it is the deprivation of maternal love and protection that hurts the most (p. 22):

> I, poor with the poorest, with none for my sorrow to care,
>> More beggared of love's daily need than of silver or gold,
> I, who only of life had hard work and hard words for my share,
>> With no home but the grave, where the heart of my mother lay cold.

In a self-reflexive relationship with the Oxford stretch of the Thames known as the River Isis, named after the great Egyptian goddess who dominated the ancient world, the girl pours out her feelings. Isis, the monumental mythic mother-figure known in Greece as Demeter (mother, sister, or spouse of Osiris-Dionysus – or even all three), has been seen as an early model for representations of the Virgin Mother and Child:

> Statues of the Egyptian goddess Isis holding the divine child have been the models for many Christian representations of Mary and the baby Jesus. They are so like those of the Madonna and child that they have sometimes received the adoration of ignorant Christians. Statues of the black virgin, so highly venerated in certain French cathedrals during the Middle Ages have proved upon examination to be basalt statues of Isis![29]

Of Isis, Margot K. Louis (referring to her in her Greek form as Demeter, mother of the goddess Koré – also known as Persephone or Proserpine) writes: 'The Mysteries of Eleusis, which celebrated Demeter and Persephone and may have re-enacted their story, promised eternal life.

So did Christianity.'[30] Yet Louis points out that during the latter half of the nineteenth century poets such as Algernon Swinburne used poems about Proserpine to challenge Christianity and help 'foster the pessimism of the fin-de-siècle [which] became popular in England'.[31] Louis quotes from Swinburne's 'Notes on Poems and Reviews' (1866) in which he describes his poem 'The Garden of Proserpine' as a dramatically expressive lyric that conveys 'the brief total pause of passion and of thought' (after 'tempestuous pleasures') when 'the spirit, without fear or hope of good things or evil, hungers and thirsts only after the perfect sleep'.[32] Swinburne presents Demeter's daughter, Proserpine, as a death goddess who belongs to the underworld and oblivion.

In Pfeiffer's 'From Out of the Night' the motherless girl, after a brief but passionate experience of 'tempestuous pleasures', ultimately chooses to give herself up to Isis (mother, sister, spouse of Osiris, her 'river god') – and possible oblivion.

Sex

Like Proserpine, Pfeiffer's heroine has been separated from her source of happiness, her mother. Lost, loveless, and homeless, she has had to work long hours of sweated labour just to keep herself alive. But then, one day she goes to a regatta with her friend Alice, and meets her 'river god'. From that moment everything changes (pp. 4–9):

> Stroke oar he was, the calm of gathered power upon his face
> Though flushed with coming battle to the shores of yellow hair;
> It was a lusty day of March, and this should be the race
> Whereto all England's thoughts were set. I know not by what grace
> We came to be so near – I only know that I was there . . .

> But the river, yes the river, he has got my life entwined,
> In his deadly silver meshes he has got my life in fee;
> As the flashing wings came beating up the stream against the wind,
> I turned and faced the crowd, and would have fled as flies the hind,
> But it held me while the river wrought and brought my fate to me.

During the spring the couple's romance grows more and more passionate as they float along on the River Isis. Then, in May, her young 'river god' proposes to her and their affair is consummated – and love 'breaks its sheath / With all blossoming things, and flowed forth as the waters unbound' (p. 23). Pfeiffer's vivid descriptions of love-making seem perfectly in keeping with the burgeoning spring and the shimmering charms of the Isis (p. 20):

> When the heaven being open above us, while fair at our feet
>> The pride and the joy of the earth spread a carpet of flowers,
> I went forth again with my love the glad season to greet,
>> And we rode in the triumph of Nature which seemed to be ours.
>
> How brightly you beamed on us, river, as if you took
>> In the joy that grew vocal beside you as softly we trod,
> And the voice of the love flowing forth from the deep of your heart
>> Was more full than the nightingale's own, O my young river god!

Looking back over the events, the young girl decides that everything that happened to her happened because of the river: the regatta, meeting the beautiful oarsman, falling in love with him, sexual fulfilment, becoming a fallen woman, and ending up beside the river bereft of all hope and happiness – it was all because of the River Isis.

Premonition

The young girl should have taken heed of the warning given to her when one day, thinking themselves alone, the lovers are intruded upon by a hideous old crone muttering curses (pp. 25–6):

> Yes, she stood there and faced us, a creature so haggard and bent,
>> A ruin that seemed of things sad and unholy the haunt;
> As I looked, the bright veil of the universe seemed to be rent,
>> As I heard, the shrill joy of the lark seemed an arrogant vaunt . . .
>
> Now [her lips] muttered but curses, which each to my ear was a cry,
>> While her cheek was the map of a country where cross-roads of care
> Had been ploughed through a highway of tears ere their fountain was dry,
>> And the pity of all was the ways seemed to lead nowhere . . . !

The young girl observes the old woman's cheek, criss-crossed with wrinkles like a death-map leading nowhere. Sadly the warning comes too late.

Seduction

The story, as seen through the purblind perspective of a young girl's love, glosses over the darker aspects of her seduction. Her 'river god' is the young man whose eyes scanned the crowd at the regatta, looking for a pretty face. A university student or graduate, he was on the look-out for someone just like the girl whose good looks caught his eye that day. The girl, a deprived, uneducated, emotionally needy shift-worker, though aware of the risks and dangers associated with a sexual liaison outside marriage, was blind to the oarsman's perfidy. An educated young man of superior social status, he had had all the advantages that the girl lacked and, because of this, and because he was a man with everything to gain and nothing to lose from extra-marital sex, he controlled the relationship. So this was not a relationship based on equality: far from it. This was a relationship based on deception and exploitation. The powerful young 'river god' had whispered sweet nothings into the girl's ear (p. 14):

> And he whispered me softly: 'Here love is at home, the fond tale
> Is disclosed by the glad living creatures in beauty and song,
> And our love as the love of this twain shall not falter or fail
> For the scorn of the years; they shall touch it and do it no wrong . . .'

Her 'river god' knows full well that their love is not 'at home' and that it will 'falter' and 'fail' quite soon, but he is being driven on by lust. He will say anything that will bring him closer to having sex with this naïve, working-class virgin. All through March, all through April, he has been seducing her, and now it is May and he still has not had his way with her. So he becomes bolder (p. 15):

> He had dared to make free with my heart, and had called by its name
> The secret which trembling he drew from its maidenly hold,
> And I heard unreproving, filled, thrilled with the joy and sweet shame –
> Overborne by the stress of the passion which rendered him bold.

Having raised his bid for sex to a new level but still not attained his objective, he starts to talk about marriage and she unwittingly believes him (p. 21):

> Yes, I hear him, he murmurs, 'My fair one', he calls me his queen –
> Of the May, of all Mays, and all months all the blessed year through;
> But he calls me his wife that shall be, – and the word is so keen
> That it cuts all my life, the before and thereafter, in two . . .

Then, in a 'moment of bliss' the mystery of life becomes clear to the girl who trustingly believes the young man's talk of an autumn wedding (p. 24):

> When your lips met my lips, O beloved, and the mystery first,
>> The meaning of life became clear in a moment of bliss;
> There was love at the heart of the world that had once seemed accurst,
>> And men bore not their burthens in vain if they bore them for this.

As the girl starts to imagine her wedding day, her satiated lover starts to think up ways to extricate himself from this unsuitable relationship.

Betrayal

After this consummation, it takes only a short time before his ten-page letter arrives full of excuses as to why he cannot marry her. He is too cowardly even to tell her the bad news face to face. The young girl is broken-hearted (p. 36):

> For I died by your hand in that letter; it did not require
>> Such urgence of proof that the blow was decreed and must fall;
> Ten pages – and written so fairly, and written with fire!
>> Was that well when a word of your lips had sufficed to it all?
>
> I had never contested your will, if your will was to part,
>> Neither battled nor yielded with tears as a deer brought to bay,
> I had laid all my life in your hand, had made over my heart;
>> It was easy to win me – more easy to cast me away.

As the young girl states, she has laid her life in his hands. She has given herself to him – body and soul. She has made no demands of him, yet he has cast her aside. He has satisfied his lust, so now the girl can be expunged from his life with a letter and lame excuses, and because he knows full well that she is alone with no family to comfort her, his treatment of her is even more despicable. Now a fallen woman she is shunned, even by her best friend (p. 37):

> It was Alice who was with me; we were free for half a day;
>> She, the gentlest of my workmates, held me closely by the hand,
> So she surely must have felt the shaft that struck me, if no ray
>> Of the sudden morning-glory touched her eyes or came her way;
> Yet she joins my foes and girds at him – the bitterest of the band.

The dangers of illegitimacy, of bringing fatherless babies into the world, led to the shunning of fallen women before contraception made extra-marital sex safer for them. The fallen girl describes how a 'pack' of people that she had thought of as friends finds her hiding in the church where she had sought sanctuary and, subsequently, she is hunted from place to place. The one safe place of sanctuary should have been the Church and yet the Church offers the girl no shelter. On the contrary, the Church labels the fallen girl *fornicator* while turning a blind eye to the behaviour of her lover who, with the Church's blessing, is allowed to enter the Holy State of Matrimony with another girl soon afterwards. Pfeiffer underlines the point that the selfsame Church that fails to offer sanctuary to a fallen girl gives its full blessing to the marriage of her male betrayer, thereby laying bare its blatant double standards (pp. 44–5):

> But the pack of them that came again and found me in the church,
>   And hunted me from place to place all day, yet never caught,
> Till I heard the river call, and fled, and left them in the lurch,
> And lay silent in the shadow, while they past me in their search –
>   No, I think the river never knew that it was me they sought.

Trustingly the young girl had believed her 'river god' when he proposed to her. It was only in the expectation of marriage that the girl had given herself to him. Because he was her social superior she had had faith in him, but it was because he was her social superior that he felt able to lie to her and ruin her life. Now she was on her own.

Rejection

Like Persephone released from the underworld and free to return to her mother, the young girl had thought that when she married her 'river god' she would have a mother again. She dreamed of the warm and loving embrace of a mother-in-law who would fill the aching void in her heart, but this was not to be. The girl tells how her lover's mother rejects her and sends her straight back to the underworld in a manner so dreadful that the girl feels that the river, now her only confidante and friend, must not find out about it (p. 46):

> Hush, the river must not know that I had ever seen her face,
>   Must not know she came and found me when my torturers had fled;
> Hah! For me she had no kiss, but sat aloof in pride of race,
> Though I yearned to her – his mother – till she offered me a place

In the service of the living, never noting I was dead.

I had yearned to those cold eyes, because I saw his eyes look through,
    And, as out of frozen windows of a prison, gaze at me;
Had they softened with a tear, I think, my tears had fallen too,
And perhaps my heart in melting would have brought my life anew, –
    But to put to cruel uses – no! forbear my tears, let be!

The girl's would-be mother tries to buy her off by offering her a place in service as she confronts the girl with eyes like the 'frozen windows of a prison'. All hope is gone.

Sacrifice

The young oarsman breaks off his engagement telling the young girl that his father is sick and the family fortune has been lost. He must marry a rich woman to save his father's life and restore his family's reputation. Now a fallen woman, the girl prepares to commit suicide believing that by sacrificing her life for the life of her lover's father she can propitiate her sin and, redeemed, be able to participate with 'Him' in heaven (p. 41):

Well, a life for a life; if, when counting my treasure for loss,
    Yielding days that were priceless with love, I had seen but the eyes
Of the Christ who once suffered for men, as was said on the Cross,
    And been lifted in heart and in hope to some high paradise.

I had died not so hard; they in asking my life to redeem
    The life of another, had made me partaker with Him;
Now men sharing Christ's sorrow and death have no part in his dream,
    And his God is as lost to their love as the veiled Cherubim.

In her poem, Pfeiffer's portrayal of the fallen girl's suicide as a crucifixion is endorsed by Margaret Reynolds, who draws attention to her Christ-like self-sacrifice:

> The poem elevates the fallen woman to a saintly status, even going so far as to compare her with Christ given that she, in effect, gives her life, so that the life of her lover's father can be saved by his son's marrying a girl of a high class.[33]

That the young girl in 'From Out of the Night' feels betrayed and suffers heart-ache, anger, humiliation, and fear is understandable. But to commit suicide to propitiate the sinfulness of a love affair, and to save the life of the father of the man who betrayed you, is a response that far outweighs the demands of the circumstances. Had the young girl become pregnant suicide would be more understandable, but there is no suggestion that this was the case. If sex outside wedlock is a sin so also, according to the Church, is suicide.

Suicide

Now, building up to her suicide, the girl ruminates about the past, recounting every detail of her love affair from the moment she first saw her 'river god' until her present predicament. The girl's seduction is an old story, but beneath the girl's narrative is a subtext which, from a psychological perspective, demonstrates a profound understanding of suicide. Pfeiffer's accurate descriptions of the stages leading up to suicide – stages that were not identified until a century or more after her death – are hard to explain, although there were suicides in her family.[34] The first clinical study of suicide was carried out in France by Brierre de Boismont in 1856. Later, in 1910, Sigmund Freud and others attended one of the earliest conferences on the subject of suicide ever convened by psychoanalysts. At this meeting, Wilhelm Stekel outlined what was, until around the 1980s, considered to be the orthodox position on suicide – that suicide is the result of hostility directed towards the love object: 'No one kills himself except as he wishes the death of another'.[35] Today psychoanalysts add shame, guilt, fear, loss of autonomy, and feelings of hopelessness to the suicidal cocktail, although love and hate still remain the two main ingredients.

Conflicting feelings characterise the young girl's gradual journey towards suicide in 'From Out of the Night'. Pre-mourning her death, the girl's thoughts focus upon the mutually exclusive category of love and hate – a dichotomous logic, symptomatic of suicidal behaviour – a logic that only perceives stark alternatives.[36] It is as if the girl's thoughts are running along pre-ordained tracks towards one certain destination. Under the spell of restricted logic, the girl can see no way out of her predicament. Gradually even dichotomous logic shuts down, constricting her vision more and more. Only tunnel vision remains – a tunnel leading directly into the arms of the river she loves – and hates (p. 21):

Fill me full with sweet poison, dear river, that mingled your voice
With the words that he said when he loosened my winter of life
As the rivers are loosened in spring, when he bade me rejoice –
His Queen of the May whom the autumn should crown as his wife.

Then, as rivers are 'loosened' in the spring and flood their banks, watering and fertilising the land, so the beguiling words of the river and her 'river god' intermingled as together they tempted her. Together the river goddess Isis and her beautiful 'river god' loosened her 'winter of life' only to tighten it into a stranglehold. Now she asks the river to fill her with 'sweet poison'.

Envy

As the girl pre-mourns her death, her anguished mind rambles backwards and forwards in time. She imagines haunting the wedding of her ex-lover to his rich bride, her description now sounding like a real premonition. Referring to her lover's mother, the fallen girl comments on the ceremony (p. 46):

It was she who kissed the bride, he dared not touch her in my sight,
For he felt my ghostly presence and my shadow rise between;
But they past me by together, and she has him day and night,
With my shadow growing less and less until it dwindles quite,
Or is swallowed of her substance, and abides with him unseen.

The girl agonises in the knowledge that the rich bride will have her ex-lover 'day and night' and that, gradually, her ghostly shadow, while 'swallowed' now, will eventually be consumed by her living rival. Envy consumes the girl as she sees time working in her rival's favour. The rich wife will blossom and they will be happy together, and it will be as if she had never existed (p. 47):

And she will be a growing power and potency, the years –
The treacherous years will take her part and ravish him from me
And she will make a title out of daily smiles and tears,
And will pass to fuller blessedness through weakness which endears
And I shall be as one forbid before I cease to be.

In subsequent stanzas the girl prays – but not, as one is initially led to assume, to the Virgin Mary ('O thou blessed among women more than all of woman born!'). In fact, as gradually becomes clear, her prayers are addressed to her rival in love, the bride, beseeching her to be her comforter, her sister 'bound' by Fate. She refers to the 'web' of Fate binding herself and her rival to each other – but in this metaphor which is the spider and which the fly? The girl then expresses her anger more openly when she disturbingly conflates the bride's wedding gown with her own shroud (pp. 47–8):

> O thou blessed among women more than all of woman born!
>> Be my sister, be my comforter; nay, wherefore cold and proud?
> We are bound as in one web of Fate, the garland that was worn
> Of thee to-day, but yestereen from off my brows was torn,
>> And that costly bridal robe of thine must serve me for a shroud.
>
> Be thou high of heart as happy, leave for me a little space
>> In the silence of his thoughts, that while you pass from change
>>> to change,
> I may, balmëd with the dead, lie still with dead unchanging face,
> Making fragrant all his seasons – be this granted me for grace –
>> With some magic of the morning that might else for him grow
>>> strange.

The bride's now ghostly rival pleads with the rich wife-to-be to grant to her 'for grace' a small space in her ex-lover's thoughts so that, as she lies dead, she may bring him joy. And now addressing the lover himself, she urges him to remember how much he once loved her. She does not want every atom of her being to be lost to him. She begs to be allowed to wander in his thoughts as a ghost. She promises him no harm (pp. 48–9):

> O my love that loved me truly in the days not long ago,
>> I am young to perish wholly, let not all of me be lost;
> Take me in, and never fear me – nay, I would not work you woe;
> Keep for her the cheerful daylight, keep for her the firelight glow, –
>> Let me wander in the twilight of your thoughts, a harmless ghost.
>
> Let me steal upon your dreams, and make your broken life complete,
>> Take me in, no mortal maiden, but the spirit o[f] your youth;
> I have done with earthly longings, and their memory bitter sweet,
> And would feed you with an essence you should only taste, not eat,
>> And so keep your soul undying in its tenderness and truth.

Now 'no mortal maiden' (neither *virgin*, nor, as a result, *living*), the girl desperately clings to her earthly lover. When she says that she intends the couple no harm, the undertow of rage, resentment, and envy signals that this is not the case. There is malice in her outrageous request to steal upon the couple's dreams, to make their broken life together complete. The clues are in the words 'steal', 'broken' life, and also in her comment about the 'essence' she would feed to the couple – just a taste – to keep their souls from dying. These poisoned words spell out destruction for a couple she loathes, despite her overtures to the contrary. Now an earth-bound phantom with nothing more to lose, her destructiveness knows no bounds.

Finale

Caught up in an unendurable spiral of sorrow, the young girl is fearful of her fate when she is dead. She knows she must be punished for her sinfulness, and this means burning in the 'fiery furnace' – but then what? An undertow of impotent rage accompanies her realisation that there is no route-map for where she is going because nobody has ever returned from the 'fiery furnace' to describe their spiritual outcome. It seems that, at the very last minute, the girl starts to question her faith: does God exist? If so, is He indifferent to human suffering? Is Christianity merely a myth motivated by earthly power? The young girl believes that because her heart is too true to be cheated, she cannot cheat herself (pp. 42–3):

> Has anyone tasted my sorrow and learnt to endure,
>> Bear the curse of a Fate that knows neither design nor desert?
> But has anyone, tasting my sorrow, had proof of its cure –
>> Stood the test of the fiery furnace and come out unhurt?
>
> No, the truest of hearts fare the worst – they are hardest to cheat;
>> We are victims, not martyrs, we burn, and are calcined to stone;
> We grow black in the reek, are made bitter where once we were sweet;
>> Would my soul remain fair, it must look to the river alone.
>
> So the river – yes, the river; I have come to that at last;
>> The river is my only friend, though changed with all the rest,
> Dark and sullen, it has known me in the glory of my past
> And has smiled upon me then; for very shame it could not cast
>> Me forth if I should seek the barren haven of its breast.

Although initially the fallen girl sees her suicide as a Christ-like sacrifice, her attitude changes when she starts to consider the punishment she must endure for succumbing to the pleasures of sex. Pondering on the final outcome of her soul after she has been burnt to a cinder in the fiery furnace, she finally perceives herself to be no Christian martyr but rather the unwitting victim of a criminal untruth. The young girl also realises that throughout her tragic love affair, the only relationship that had remained constant had been her self-reflexive relationship with the River Isis. For when she had been happy, the river had sparkled; when she had been sad, the river had grown sombre. Diverging from her initial Christian stance the fallen girl decides that, however dark the Isis now seems (as compared with the shining friendliness of the past), it was her one true friend. Her spirit can only 'remain fair' if it returns to the barren, but safe, breast of her pagan soul-mate. With the final words 'O my River-God, clasp me, I come!' the girl jumps into the sullen arms of the river.

In 'From Out of the Night' Pfeiffer uses the theme of suicide to draw attention to the treatment of women by society. As a Christian, the fallen girl fears God's judgement and condemnation because of her sinfulness. She and her lover cannot marry because they come from different social classes; they cannot marry because she is poor and he needs money. She is mocked and marginalised by society because she has had sex before marriage, while he can be married in a Christian church, his reputation untarnished. Pfeiffer is drawing attention to social, sexual, and religious rules so severe that the fallen girl sees a pagan death as her only option. Turning her back on the religion that has spurned her, she surrenders her life to the pagan goddess Isis – her only friend.

In the three (very different) poems discussed in this chapter, Emily Pfeiffer draws attention to the subjection of women through procreation, motherhood, and extra-marital sex. In 'A Song of Winter' (1879), Pfeiffer links the suffering women have to endure because of their reproductive role to the suffering Jesus had to bear at his crucifixion, and in so doing presents women as exalted, spiritual beings. In 'Madonna Dūnya' (1879), she combines images of a peasant mother with those of the Virgin Mother in order to release each from the patriarchal prejudices restricting their lives. The apparent fusion of the two mothers into a single spiritual entity – an entity subsequently transported to heaven by Elijah – may be an attempt on Pfeiffer's part to restore to the Mother of God (the Maker and Creator of the Universe) the power denied her by the Church. Finally, in 'From Out of the Night' (1882), Pfeiffer draws attention to prevailing nineteenth-century double standards. These are social, in the form of class distinction; religious, in terms of the institutionalised patriarchy of the Church; and sexual, in punishing women for expressing their sexuality while condoning the same behaviour in their male partners. Ultimately the fallen woman turns her back on Christianity and commits her life (or death) to the river goddess, Isis.

At once characteristic of her experimental facility with form and genre, and of the complexity of her engagement with her cause, Pfeiffer's blank-verse novel *Glân-Alarch, His Silence and Song* (1877), published five years before 'From Out of the Night', treats the subjects of suicide and paganism from a different perspective – as the following chapter will argue.

Notes

1. Elizabeth Barrett Browning, 'Lessons from the Gorse' [1841], *Poetical Works*, op. cit., p. 299. Barrett Browning uses the image of the gorse to teach 'us' to be strong, glad, and humble. In the second stanza her words read: 'Set as lights upon a hill, / Tokens to the wintry earth that Beauty liveth still!'. Compare Pfeiffer, 'A Song of Winter', stanza seven: 'And yet thy lamp upon the hill . . .' (p. 97).

2. Adelaide Procter, 'A Tomb in Ghent' [1855], in *Complete Works* (London: George Bell, 1905), p. 67.

3. Christina Rossetti, 'My Dream', in *Complete Works*, ed. R. W. Crump (London: Penguin, 2005), p. 33.

4. Emily Pfeiffer, *Quarterman's Grace and Other Poems* (London: Kegan Paul, 1879), p. 97.

5. John Stuart Mill, *The Subjection of Women* [1869] (London: Penguin Classics, 2006), pp. 165–6.

6. Kimberly VanEsveld Adams, 'The Madonna and Anna Jameson', in *Woman's Theology in Nineteenth Century Britain: Transfiguring the Faith of Their Fathers*, ed. Julie Melnyk (London: Garland, 1998), pp. 59–82 (p. 77).

7. Anna Jameson, *Legends of the Madonna, as Represented in the Fine Arts* [1852] (London: Unit Library, 1903), Introduction, p. 4.

8. Ibid., pp. 4–5.

9. Anne Clifford, *Introducing Feminist Theology* (New York: Orbis, 2001), p. 187.

10. Joseph Pohle, Arthur Preuss, *Mariology: A Dogmatic Treatise on the Blessed Virgin Mary, Mother of God*, 2nd edn (London: B. Herder, 1916), pp. 5–6.

11. Julia Kristeva, 'Stabat Mater', in *The Kristeva Reader*, ed. Toril Moi (Oxford: Blackwell, 1986), pp. 161–2.

12. Marina Warner, *Alone of All Her Sex: Myth and Cult of the Virgin Mary* (London: Vintage, 1976), Prologue, p. 23.

13. Ibid., p. 50.

14. Waldemar Januszczak, 'Art Under Attack', *Sunday Times* (6 October 2013).

15. Ibid.

16. Emily Pfeiffer, *Quarterman's Grace*,, pp. 59–76.

17. Jane Ellen Harrison, *Alpha and Omega* (London: Sidgwick & Jackson Ltd., 1915), pp. 202–3.

18. See Emily Pfeiffer, *Women and Work* (London: 1888): 'It would be invidious to mention . . . women who have been working [for the Suffrage League] . . . for more than thirty years. [They] have laboured through the toil and heat of the day; they have braved ridicule, and even disgust. They have done . . . as best they were able' (pp. 173–4).

19. Margaret Bruzelius, 'Mother's Pain, Mother's Voice: Gabriela Mistral, Julia Kristeva, and the Mater Dolorosa', *Tulsa Studies in Women's Literature*, 18.2 (1999), 215–33 (p. 220).

20. Ibid.

21. Emily Pfeiffer, *Under the Aspens, Lyrical and Dramatic* (London: Kegan Paul, Trench, 1882), pp. 1–50.

22. See Angela Leighton and Margaret Reynolds, eds, *Victorian Women Poets: An Anthology* (Oxford: Blackwell 1991) , p. 277.

23. D'Amico, op. cit., p. 70.

24. Adelaide Procter, *Legends and Lyrics* (London: Bell & Daldy, 1858).

25. Elizabeth Barrett Browning, *Poetical Works*, op. cit., pp. 374-539.

26. See Reynolds and Leighton, eds., *Victorian Women Poets*, p. 433.

27. Sarah Dana Greenough, *Mary Magdalene, A Poem* (Boston, USA: James R. Osgood and Company, 1880).

28. Amy Levy, *A Minor Poet And Other Verse* (London: 1884); Mathilde Blind, *Dramas in Miniature* (London, 1891).

29. Timothy Freke and Peter Gandy, *The Jesus Mysteries* (London: Thorsons, 1999), p. 114.

30. Louis, op. cit., p. 71.

31. Ibid., pp. 57–8.

32. Ibid., p. 59, citing Swinburne, *Complete Works*, ed. Sir Edmund Gosse and Thomas James Wise, 20 vols (1925–7), 16, 361–2.

33. Margaret Reynolds, op. cit., p. 339.

34. According to an article in *Collections Historical and Archaeological relating to Montgomeryshire and its Borders* 49 (1940), 258, a Welsh relation of Emily Pfeiffer committed suicide, as documented: 'By him, who died by his own hand, as a result, it is said, of a failure of the firm [Blayney, Tilsley & Blayney of Newtown].'

35. Edwin Schneidman, *Voices of Death* (London: Bantam Books, 1982), pp. 42–4. Schneidman, a suicidologist, lists the findings of investigations made in the nineteenth and twentieth centuries, referring to Paul Friedman, ed., *On Suicide* (New York: International Universities Press, 1967).

36. Ibid., pp. 42–3.

CHAPTER THREE

Integrating Mythologies

IN HER BLANK-VERSE NOVEL *Glân-Alarch, His Silence and Song* (1877), Emily Pfeiffer reconstructs history, myth, and legend to create a mythic woman saviour of the Welsh people.[1] By subverting conventional narratives, and by blurring and blending Christian and pagan imagery, Pfeiffer creates a heroine who, through her sacrifice and suicide, becomes the catalyst for a great Welsh victory against invading Saxons. A mortal carrying signs of death upon her face, Pfeiffer's heroine is both 'the highest dweller upon the earth' and 'a disembodied soul made free of the unlovely flesh'. Yet despite all this, she marries the man she loves and lives happily ever after.

In this poetic, 'mythopoeic', work, Emily Pfeiffer rearranges a series of kaleidoscopic images from the mists of Celtic pre-history in order to inform her nineteenth-century readers about a matter close to her heart.[2] In presenting contrasting images of her heroine, and using these images to suggest new spiritual possibilities for women, Pfeiffer demonstrates her technical brilliance in this tale of Celtic valour.

The Appropriation of King Arthur

In her Preface to *Glân-Alarch*, Emily Pfeiffer writes:

> I have chosen a remote historic epoch for my subject; but in dealing with it, I have tried to penetrate beneath the veil of chivalry, which, however fair, I feel to be still a veil, to the homelier life which it in part conceals from us; and by the help of the few facts we possess, and the indications supplied by race, to revivify a typical moment of that past which lies

at the root of the present through which we are living, and the future to which we aspire.[3]

With these words Pfeiffer declares her intention to revivify a typical moment in history as a lens through which to examine some, as yet undisclosed, nineteenth-century issue that has implications for the future. By setting her novel in the dim and distant past (possibly around the sixth century AD), Pfeiffer has a free hand to construct a story to suit her own purposes. Creating her own version of events, and expressing them through the masculine tones of Glân-Alarch, a respected Welsh bard and seer, the 'moment' Pfeiffer chooses for revivification proves to be far from typical.

The bard Glân-Alarch describes the anxiety of Prince Eurien of Garth who, faced with possible annihilation at the hands of Saxon invaders, yearns for King Arthur to come back from the 'land of Faëry' to repeat the Welsh victories of the past. Confiding his fears to Glân-Alarch, Prince Eurien looks back nostalgically to the halcyon days of 'Dux Bellorum' (p. 115):

> 'Think you in truth that he, – our great Pendragon, –
> Arthur, still lives in some high land of Faëry
> Whence he may win to us, and with that brand
> Men tell of, cleave the heart of Dynas-Emrys,
> And mount the golden chair which Merlin guards
> Within? What say you? will he once more gather
> Our scattered Cymri in his kingly hands,
> Bind them in one, and so compacted hurl them –
> Hurl them against the Saxon that we back him,
> Ay, back until we choke him in the sea?'

Although the historic King Arthur has proved elusive, the legendary King Arthur has fully compensated for any lack of factual evidence. 'Whatever grain of truth this story may have possessed has been hopelessly obscured,' comment Laurie Finke and Martin Shichtman, pointing out that the two historical works referring to King Arthur – *Historia Brittonum* (c. 829–30 AD), written in Latin in Gwynedd in North Wales, and the *Annales Cambriae*, written in Dyfed around 953–54 AD – are each variously unreliable.[4] Finke and Shichtman nevertheless concede that historians are reluctant to write off the existence of King Arthur altogether. In addition, they observe the way in which historical narratives about King Arthur's military successes tend to re-emerge at critical moments in history:

> We contend that King Arthur has been used by historians – medieval and modern – as a potent but empty signifier to which meaning could be attached that served to legitimate particular forms of political authority and cultural imperialism'.[5]

Notable among the historians discussed by Finke and Shichtman stands Winston Churchill, whose glorification of King Arthur in World War Two was part of an overall bid to unite the British nation against a fascist aggressor. But what motivated Emily Pfeiffer to appropriate and glorify King Arthur in her 1870s verse novel *Glân-Alarch*? If the legend was used 'to legitimate particular forms of political authority and cultural imperialism', which of these did she intend it to 'legitimate', and why? Finke and Shichtman question Churchill's war-time reference to the slaughter of 'innumerable hosts of foul barbarians' using language that they consider disturbing.[6] Yet Pfeiffer uses similarly disturbing language when Glân-Alarch describes an incident to which she gives great dramatic prominence. This incident occurs when Prince Eurien is addressing his men in the great hall – when suddenly (pp. 35–6):

> A knight on horseback, pale and sad as death,
> And misty as a spectre in the smoke
> Wreathing his charger, rode into the hall
> And struck his spear with force upon the flags . . .

With sobs and curses the knight tells Prince Eurien and his assembled men that a band of marauding Saxons has perpetrated a massacre at a nearby monastery. Glân-Alarch's outrage at this atrocity is palpable (pp. 37–8):

> Twelve hundred monks of Bangor, men of God,
> His ministers that were, his martyrs now, –
> Slain at His altar, – slain before His eyes,
> Kneeling to ask for judgment of their cause
> There where their butchers were as free to kneel,
> But that they dared not tempt high god in face.
> Twelve hundred martyrs! . . .
> Slain by the sword, who never took the sword,
> Slaughtered like lambs at pasture on the hills!

The brutal Saxon, Ethelfrith, the leader
Of the vile scum . . .

Glân-Alarch's reference to these men as 'butchers', 'brutal Saxon', and 'vile scum' uses language similar to that used by Churchill in his reference to the 'innumerable hosts of foul barbarians' that bombed Britain in the war. Both Churchill and Pfeiffer's speaker, Glân-Alarch – claiming Christ on their side – feel justified in using defamatory language against a hostile invader. Applying a postcolonial perspective to her study of *Glân-Alarch*, Catherine Brennan suggests that Pfeiffer uses the word 'Saxon' (or, in Welsh, *Saeson*) as an umbrella term for both the early Saxon colonisers of England and also the nineteenth-century English imperialist oppressors of Wales.[7] If that is the case, and in the light of Finke's and Shichtman's theories, Pfeiffer may have appropriated the legend of King Arthur in order to vilify the 'political authority' and 'cultural imperialism' imposed upon the Welsh people by nineteenth-century 'Saxon' rule. Yet Brennan makes no reference to the role of King Arthur in the verse novel, nor does she mention the fact that the indigenous tribes of what became 'Angle-land' (or England) had been subject to the same 'processes of physical and legislative brutality' from Germanic invaders as the Welsh but had, ultimately, been defeated.[8] The defeated Brythonic Celts of 'England' were either killed, or absorbed into Saxon communities, or forced out into remote pockets of the North and West.

Although Emily Pfeiffer's mother was Welsh, her father was an Englishman and her husband was a German, so I question the extent to which Pfeiffer deployed *Glân-Alarch, His Silence and Song* as a vehicle for criticising nineteenth-century English imperialism. If it was her intention to conflate the two periods of history (by equating the Germanic pagans who invaded Wales in Celtic pre-history with the Christian imperialists ruling Wales in the nineteenth century), then it follows that Glân-Alarch's epithets – 'vile scum', 'brutal Saxon', and 'butchers' – apply as much to nineteenth-century English imperialists as to the sixth-century Saxon hordes.[9] Is this what Pfeiffer meant in her Preface when she referred to the 'typical moment of the past which lies at the root of the present through which we are living, and the future to which we aspire'? Is this what Pfeiffer wanted *Glân-Alarch* to disclose?

Pfeiffer could not have been unaware of the political and cultural parallels she was drawing between the two periods in Welsh history, but I do not think that this was her main objective in writing this extensive verse novel. For one thing, in her Preface, she draws the attention to her adoption of Irish term 'Sassenach' instead of using the Welsh term 'Saeson', thereby making it clear that she did not wish to offend her English readership. In addition, she describes Prince Eurien facing – albeit in microcosm – a set of circumstances not dissimilar to those facing Churchill prior to World War Two. The enemy is knocking at the door and the chances of survival are slim. Moreover, when Prince Eurien speaks to his tribal leaders it becomes worryingly apparent that he is no 'Dux Bellorum'. So what is the purpose of linking the Arthurian legend to this particular slice of Welsh pseudo-history? For what reason does Pfeiffer laud King Arthur's military prowess at the expense of Prince Eurien? In attempting to answer these questions, I turn to the final paragraph of *King Arthur and the Myth of History* where Finke and Shichtman conclude that the Arthurian legends were given a place in history because 'they could contain and advance culturally useful agendas'.[10] And here I think we come to the crux of the question of Pfeiffer's motivation when, in her Preface, she writes: 'I have tried to penetrate beneath the veil of chivalry, which, however fair, I feel to be still a veil, to the homelier life which it in part conceals from us.' Pfeiffer, penetrating beneath the veil of chivalry – in both its medieval military sense, and its nineteenth-century metaphorical application – appropriates and exploits the myth of King Arthur in order to advance an emancipationist agenda that is even more important to her than English imperialism. To this end, I argue, Pfeiffer constructed her blank-verse novel to create a heroine of Arthurian proportions – a powerful and mighty war-leader who snatches Wales from the jaws of defeat – and her name is Mona.[11]

Mona

Emily Pfeiffer constructs her multi-faceted heroine through the perception of Glân-Alarch, the bard and seer. Early in the poem, Glân-Alarch describes an incident when, high up in the Welsh mountains, he hears the sound of a hymn being sung. Although he cannot see the singer, his heart is filled with intense joy. Then, when the hymn-singer emerges from the mist, he sees her as a mountain queen, 'sceptered and crowned', 'a gliding phantom of our hills'. These two images – Christian and pagan – quickly morph into another image: that of a young girl with blue eyes who, removing flowers from a homemade crown, shyly presses back her hair. A Christian hymn-singer, a pagan spirit of the hills, and a shy girl roaming the mountains with her dog, Mona is a complex Celtic character. Glân-Alarch describes his mystical experience (pp. 12–13):

> And as I listened thus, I heard a song . . .
> A hymn in which the lark's clear-gushing joy
> Was married to a mood which had been born
> Of shadow-haunted mountain tarns, and rocks
> Which glacier drifts had furrowed, and of peaks
> Which point from age to age their cones to heaven
> And topple down from age to age to earth.
>
> And hearing of the song, I saw a shade
> That glided towards us on the rolling mist;
> A vast and regal shade as of a queen
> Sceptered and crowned, – and thought that clarion hymn
> Whose joyance all too keen, broke like a wail,
> Became this gliding phantom of our hills . . .
>
> There met us face to face, no mountain queen
> Of mould majestic, but a lithe, spare sprite,
> Our maiden Mona, singing as she came,
> And looking up above our heads, with eyes
> Whose gaze appeared as though it came from far,
> And pierced yet farther through the widening blue.
>
> The crown upon her head was of white
> And purple mountain heather, and her wand
> An ashen branch, with berries at its point;
> Her blood-hound, Myneth, joyful at the touch
> Of Mona's hand . . .

Glân-Alarch, responding to Mona's hymn-singing, clearly sees her as spiritually gifted; but to what extent is she Christian and to what extent pagan? Margot K. Louis draws attention to the ways mythography 'informed and was informed by wider cultural developments: the great and difficult project of replacing the Christian mythos that for so long formed the imaginative core of Western culture'.[12] Louis observes a growing 'insistence' during the century that 'the mythology of the ancient Greeks (specifically, that of Homer) [was] less deeply, less truly religious than the Mystery cults of the chthonian deities Persephone, Dionysos, and Adonis', and that this 'opposition between myth and Mystery . . . grew out of Christian and Romantic concepts of spiritual experience':[13]

> British mythographers were hampered . . . by the need to conciliate a strong evangelical lobby deeply suspicious of paganism in any form. Romantic and Victorian poetry, however, offered a field in which myth could be used, revised, and even explicitly discussed with more freedom than was available to scholars at the time. Poets were not entirely exempt from evangelical pressure, but poetry was to a large extent protected by its traditional association with myth and by the symbolic mode developed in the Romantic era.[14]

By the time Pfeiffer published *Glân-Alarch* in 1877, mythography was leaning towards the Greek 'Mystery' religions at the expense of both Greek mythology and the orthodox Christian theology, and it seems that Pfeiffer exploited this growing spiritual confusion to advance her emancipationist cause.

Having introduced Mona as an Irish Christian with pagan overtones, Pfeiffer now depicts her as a powerful war-leader who goads the Welsh to stand up and fight. Learning of the murder of the Welsh monks at Bangor by pagan invaders, Mona directly opposes Prince Eurien's wait-and-see policy as she abandons the women of the royal household, and her loom, and steps forward to confront Eurien and his tribal chiefs. She takes up her harp and, overcoming her shyness, sings out with bardic fire – a veritable Cyridwen (the fabled Celtic goddess of rebirth). Glân-Alarch observes (pp. 42–3):

> It was not Mona
> Who turned the eyes which had become as wells
> Of awful depth . . . no, not she, our merle,
> But dread Cyridwen, genius of our race,
> Descended there to front us with our shame . . .
> She lifted from her side her Irish harp,
> When from beneath her fingers there broke forth
> A wail which matched the message of her eyes.

Upon hearing Mona's voice Weroc, one of Prince Eurien's more churlish tribesmen, utters an oath and tries to stop Mona's 'song' – but she halts him in his tracks merely by putting her arm out. Mona's power is immense, as she taunts the men (pp. 44–5):

> 'They have hunted you to your hills, ye men of Glyneth!
> Your rivers and plains are the spoil of the Sassenach;
> And they laugh like slaves in the face of him that winneth . . .'

> 'You have fattened for them your fields, ye men of Glyneth,
> Your dead have covered the soil as a fruitful flood,
> And the rivers that dance in the sun and look not back,
> Are fuller for tears, and richer for running blood . . .'

Mona finishes her long rallying cry with a final dig aimed at Eurien and his chiefs (pp. 47–8):

> 'Forget your olden glory, ye men of Glyneth,
> Cast the torch from the armed right hand ere it flickers or fails,
> Stamp it out and end the story, O men of Glyneth,
> Let Cambria fall like a stronghold that treason assails,
> And in tears of your shame shall your land be re-christened wild
> Wales.'

Glân-Alarch, as interpreter of Mona's song, links her rallying cry to the demise of the Brythonic Celt which he personifies as a mangled body torn limb from limb by the Saxon foe, its extremities kept alive by the 'bleeding heart' of Welsh nationalism. Pushed to the 'sad corners of the earth', the life of the surviving Celtic nations depends upon a Welsh victory. Glân-Alarch says of Mona (p. 48):

> Wales, Wales, wild Wales! Her hearers knew full well
> The land she sung of was the bleeding heart
> Of Britain, Britain mangled by the foe,
> Torn limb from limb, the parts still quick with life,
> Throbbing in all sad corners of the earth.

As Mona leaves the hall she turns back, raising trembling hands and tearful eyes towards her beloved Eurien who returns her gaze with a look of 'displeasure' as if 'he in taking back a wandering slave / Had marked her that she might not stray again'. She hears him say to his men:

'Beseech you, friends, give quittance for her youth
And scanty knowledge of the ways of men,
Which, were her early baptism of blood,
Hath wrought her fervid soul to such high pitch
As borders on distemper, that at whiles
She oversteps those bounds which God has set,
And men approve becoming in a maid.'

Prince Eurien's response is to cut Mona down to size. He asks his men to make allowances for her youth and ignorance: she does not understand the ways of the court, and she has had a difficult childhood. The violence of her childhood in Ireland, the bloody death of her father at the hands of the Vikings, and her years living as an orphan on the island of Mona, have made her highly strung to the point of hysteria. She has overstepped her position as a woman who must submit to masculine power – such bold behaviour being unfeminine and unattractive. Although he loves Mona, Prince Eurien is embarrassed by her passionate outburst in front of his men – an outburst that has unintentionally highlighted his inadequacies as a war-leader. He is no King Arthur – but Mona is.

Suicide and Sacrifice

After Eurien's rebuke Mona flees the hall and climbs high up the mountainside to be alone with 'Mother Nature' – but she has been followed by the wicked widow, Bronwen. Mona hears laboured breathing below her (p. 55):

Then saw the sleek, preened head of Bronwen, rising
Slowly above the rock, and the two eyes
That caught a stonier glitter meeting hers,
Closing upon her while the face recoiled, –
Shrunk back, – as might have shrunk the small barbed head
Of some fair-painted beast before it struck.

The widow has designs on Mona – her youth, her power, her happy betrothal to Prince Eurien – Bronwen wants all this for herself. So she follows Mona up the mountain in order to rid herself of her rival. This she does by telling Mona a string of lies. Firstly she tells Mona that Prince Eurien has banished her from Garth for speaking out against him in court. Then she informs Mona that she and Prince Eurien are in love with each other, and when Mona cries out: 'He loves me!' Bronwen replies: 'Child, he loves you as his hound, / Stroking your head when you have served him well' (p. 66). Too naïve to realise that Bronwen is lying, Mona's shock and distress pushes her into a terrible state of mental anguish. Everything Bronwen has said has the ring of truth, and so Mona decides to sacrifice her life so that Prince Eurien and Bronwen can be happy together (p. 73):[15]

> Then her eyes
> Swept the horizon's verge, and felt the world
> A desert of all howling miseries,
> And with her hands she warned it off from her, –
> The weird, wild world, and bright calm woman there
> Who mocked her with the beauty that he loved, –
> She pushed it from her, and her steps recoiled –
> A shriek! – It was not Mona, – she was gone,
> Gone from the giddy verge, gone, gone from pain,
> And giddiness of unprepared act,
> Caught up! Yea, God, I say it yet again,
> Caught up from her despair, caught up by Thee,
> Rapt, lifted by Thine arm, great God for whom
> There is nor high nor low, above, beneath,
> Darkness or death, but only light and love!

Pfeiffer here deliberately repeats the words 'Caught up' (by God) to emphasise a happy spiritual outcome for Mona, but Glân-Alarch, upon learning of her death, is so overwhelmed with grief that he loses his bardic gift of 'Song' and becomes 'Silent'. Yet his description of Mona as a Christian, a pagan, a bard, a war-leader, and a girl who sacrifices her life for the man she loves is not yet complete: there is another facet to Mona's character which Glân-Alarch finds out about later in the narrative.

The Appropriation of St Melangell

With Mona dead, Glân-Alarch silent, Bronwen married to Prince Eurien, and the Saxons ready to invade Wales, Prince Eurien seems trapped in a state of mental paralysis. Unable to decide a clear course of action, he and his men pass the time in sporting activities. One day, after returning from one of his hunting expeditions, Eurien tells Glân-Alarch about a strange incident that occurred while he and his men were coursing a hare. Round and round they circled in pursuit until Eurien found himself alone with the hounds. Then the hare doubled back on its tracks and Eurien blew his horn as the hounds, yelping, flung themselves over the brook. Eurien followed alone (pp. 127–8):

> 'Glân-Alarch! From the side of Gant-y-Wennol,
> Letting itself fall slowly, as a giant
> Folding his arms round peaks and crags, might drop
> From off a mountain's brow, there came a cloud, –
> A tall, white cloud, which spread itself in mist,
> Over the path we followed through the vale . . .'

At first Eurien notices nothing unusual about the tall, white cloud. He pursues the hare back and forth until eventually the hare is exhausted and lies down on the ground waiting to be killed by the hounds (pp. 128–9):

> 'We gained upon the hare; again she broke . . .
> She lay down spent; she yielded, poor dumb wretch,
> But yielded to fierce foes who gave no quarter . . .
> But lo, within the mist whereof we neared
> The skirts, there stood revealed now to view
> A maiden, draped, and veiled in spotless white, –
> A maid of stature tall and vast of limb,
> Beyond the wont of mortals; and she seemed
> Of the white mist to be the whiter core.

> 'Ah then, Glân-Alarch mine, a weird, a wonder,
> Grew up before my eyes; this stately virgin,
> This maiden of the mist, spread her fair arms,
> And into them, half dead, our victim sprung, –
> Sprung with an impulse of expiring nature, –
> And panting on a heart that seemed the home
> Of all the charities, closed her faint eyes,
> And drooped her head in sweet abandonment,
> And utter joy of safety, and of rest . . .

>   'At the foot
> Of that strange presence white and cold, they fell, –
> They fell, – their tongues subdued to tremulous sounds,
> Tamed in a moment . . .'

A maid veiled in spotless white, tall, and vast beyond any mortal dimension, emerges from the mist. Eurien describes how 'this stately virgin' spreads out her arms and the female hare leaps into them for protection.

Pfeiffer's depiction of a hare being rescued by a young maiden is based on a legend which is said to have occurred in sixth-century Montgomeryshire. Pfeiffer, raised in that county, would have been familiar with the story of Melangell and the hare – a legend she appropriates in *Glân-Alarch*, not only because it offers her emancipationist fantasy the solidity of a real historical time-frame but also because it enables her to align the pagan and supernatural elements of her portrayal of Mona with the more acceptable Christian attributes of a real Celtic saint.

Melangell, the daughter of an Irish king, came to Montgomeryshire around the sixth century where she lived as a contemplative, sleeping on the bare rock. According to legend, Brochfael Ysgythrog, Prince of Montgomeryshire, while hunting a hare, followed his hounds through a thicket of thorns to find a girl lying on a rock lost in contemplation. The hare was hiding under the hem of her garment. The hounds were instantly pacified, leaving the hare untouched. Moved by Melangell's saintliness, Prince Brochfael bestowed on her the valley as a place of sanctuary. Later Melangell became Abbess of a religious community there, and today the Church of St Melangell is still a place of pilgrimage. Records suggest that Melangell could have died as early as 590 AD, which makes her roughly contemporary with the action of *Glân-Alarch*. Today the hare is still a protected animal in Cwm Pennant, and carvings of hares can still be seen above the rood beam in the church. The Celtic patron of animals and natural environments, St Melangell represents reverence for all living things and, moving in the same intellectual milieu as the nascent anti-vivisectionists, Pfeiffer would have found Melangell a compelling template for the characterisation of Mona. In addition, the hare – a pagan symbol – has suitably mystical associations.

Clearly this maiden 'tall and vast of limb, / Beyond the wont of mortals' is Mona. Yet, strangely, instead of being amazed to see this vast apparition of the girl he loved and to whom he had been betrothed for three years, Prince Eurien falls to the ground in abject shame vowing never to hunt hares again (p. 129):

'I fell,
I too, upon my knees, and could have buried
My shamed manhood in the dust with them.'

Eurien's reaction feels unconvincing: Pfeiffer is clearly making some other point here. It seems possible that she purposely appropriated the legend of St Melangell in order to make feminist points – to contrast the masculine hunter and destroyer of nature with the feminine protector and promoter of nature. Around 1877, when *Glân-Alarch* was published, women such as Pfeiffer's friend, the theist Frances Power Cobbe (1822–1904), belonged to a group that saw the anti-vivisection campaign as symbolic of two opposing visions of human progress: masculine power and intellect on one side, feminine love and nurturing on the other. The former, patriarchal vision of human progress promulgated by Judaeo-Christian religion accords mankind 'dominion . . . over every living thing that moveth upon the earth' (Genesis 1:28), and the Church has a sporadic involvement in savage acts against animals. Arthur Findlay, writing at the start of the Second World War, describes the French Feast of St Hubert, patron saint of hunting. Before the hunt there is a religious service and the priest blesses the hounds: '[Then they are] set loose on a defenceless stag in a park from which it is unable to escape.'[16] Findlay adds: 'The mentality which sees nothing wrong in making animals suffer is on a similar level to the mentality that believes in orthodox Christianity, and, just as the belief in Christian creeds and doctrines declines, so does humanitarianism increase'.[17] According to Findlay, reverence for all life increases as Christian orthodoxy decreases, and yet Pfeiffer, raised on Christian creeds and doctrines, depicts Mona as a personification of St Melangell – a young woman so concerned with the life of one hunted hare that she returns to earth in spirit form to save its life.

Miracles

It seems that Mona has returned from the dead to save the life of a hunted hare, but this is not her only reappearance. On one occasion Glân-Alarch sees Mona standing close to Eurien at a feast at Garth, her face uplifted as she gazes into his eyes. Glân-Alarch now realises that she has been sent by God to save the Welsh from Saxon invasion (pp. 169–70):

> Then knew I she was come
> God-sent to speed the battle for a soul
> Against the powers of Cythraul, and my heart

> Grew pure of hate and fear in looking on her –
> God's minister, free of the gate of death,
> God's maiden soldier, who was panoplied
> In purity alone, bearing no weapon
> Saving her tempered sword of virgin love.

Glân-Alarch sees Mona again, although Eurien, struggling to come to grips with impending war, seems blind to 'the heavenly vision of our vanished Mona' (pp. 170–2):

> And all this while it stood, –
> The heavenly vision of our vanished Mona, –
> With looks meseemed of all too-human sorrow
> For one who was a visitor to earth
> From Gwynfyd, sphere of utter joy in love . . .
> When all were sat again I sought the place
> Of the white soul of Mona. It was gone.

Later, however (p. 174), Prince Eurien does see Mona. He tells Glân-Alarch:

> 'And I, Glân-Alarch, followed with mine eyes
> His gaze, and in the ghostly, sheeted moonbeams
> Gleaming without the oriel, they alighted
> Upon that same white spirit which late had looked
> On Eurien from the table, – Mona's spirit –
> The sad, wide eyes o'ercharged with love and tears
> Seeming to let their treasure overflow
> And glorify her face, baptising it
> With sorrow touched with purest light of heaven.'

Glân-Alarch notices a change in the demeanour of Prince Eurien who, freed of fear, tells him that Mona has returned to save him – and Wales (pp. 177–8):

> 'She lives, Glân-Alarch; I have looked on her,
> Have heard her voice; she lives for Wales and me;
> Love will not let her spirit free of us, –
> Death cannot hold her, – love has conquered it!
>
> There I saw her stand,
> When at the feast, where I had lost myself,
> She found me with her eyes. Glân-Alarch mine,
> How knew you that the dead could speak to us?
> My eyes, my ears, are open now as yours.'

Eurien's life was saved, he tells Glân-Alarch, when he was caught up in a black cloud on Crag-Eyrie. One false move to either side and he would have fallen to his death, but Mona's voice at his side whispered softly and repeatedly: 'Follow, Eurien, follow . . . Eurien, follow, Eurien'(p. 179). By yielding to Mona's voice, Eurien had been led safely over the deadly ridge of Crib-y-dysgull. Yet when close to Garth he heard Mona's voice speaking to him again – but this time the words were changed: 'Teudric and Tintern' (p. 180). Mona's voice has reinforced his own tentative plan to ask ex-King Teudric, the royal hermit of the Wye (and putative descendant of King Arthur), to lead the Welsh in battle.

Later, Prince Eurien and his men march south to join Teudric in a great battle to save Wales from the Saxon hordes. Glân-Alarch is too old to fight, yet he is able to follow events through a series of visions. In one of these he sees Saxons burning down the house where Bronwen has fled with her baby. Glân-Alarch fears for the safety of Eurien's son, but then in a vision (p. 227):

> I heard the step,
> I saw the shape, I felt the seraph wings,
> And knew the babe was saved; safe too that maid
> Whom nature loved and feared; – I saw no more.

Bronwen has been raped and murdered by a Saxon, and Eurien, stricken with anxiety for his baby's safety, hears his name spoken (pp. 241–2):

> And Eurien in that moment
> Knows that his infant's head is safely shrined
> Upon that heart whereto the harried hare
> Had fled for refuge, as to some known altar
> Reared in a chosen temple of high God.
> And more than this: he knows that that white maid
> Who looms so largely through the mist, and this
> On whose frail limbs the smell and smoke of fire
> Still linger, is the same brave, earth-clad soul,
> No fleshless spirit unassailable,
> But Mona as she was, – the highest dweller
> Upon the earth, but still on earth a dweller.

Glân-Alarch is overjoyed that 'She has . . . come again with, on her mortal face, / The lingering glory of the blessed dead'. Eurien welcomes

Mona back into his heart and home, and later Glân-Alarch refers to her as 'a virgin mother, loved of him who owns the service of all hearts' (p. 246).

Mona's Explanations

Pfeiffer, having described Mona as a disembodied apparition working to snatch the Welsh from the jaws of defeat (and to save the life of a hunted hare), now presents her living in a neighbouring valley. It transpires that Mona – like Melangell perhaps – has been living as a hermit since her fall off the mountainside. Mona provides Glân-Alarch with two completely contradictory versions of her suicide. The first supports the idea that she was sent as an emissary from God to save the Welsh Christians from pagan overthrow (pp. 194–6):

> 'I was saved, Glân-Alarch, –
> Made free of the unlovely flesh, which still
> Had been to him a bond or a reproach,
> And set to do him service as a spirit,
> And as a disembodied soul, to grow
> Dear, more lovely in the light of thought,
> Yet dwell with him on the same place of being,
> And breathe with him the sweet air of the world; –
> Saved as by a miracle, from the base joy
> Of living as a beggar on his bounty, –
> A beggar with one plea, that I was blind; –
> Saved, saved from this, to do the thing whereto
> My spirit, poorly housed was sent by God:
> To watch him as his shadow, and to gather
> Here, in the silence of my hidden life,
> God's message in the wind and in the stars,
> And bear him when his senses are perturbed
> By grosser clamour of his working days . . .
> I learnt the truth of Bronwen; it was truth
> Which then she spoke; would God she knew no other!
> My love was not a flower to grace his life;
> I stood before him as a rod, which never
> Would blossom in his hand.'

With these words, Mona clearly states that after she died she returned in spirit form as God's emissary to help the Welsh in their fight against the Saxons. She then recounts another version of her suicide (pp. 196–7):

> 'I fell
> And falling grasped unknowingly, the sapling
> Which grows from out the rock where it breaks off . . .
> In rising, as an arrow from a bow, –
> Shot clear of danger from the jutting crags,
> And dropped into the tallest of those trees
> That rise from out the stunted grove there striving
> Towards Clogwyn Cromlech.
> 'When I woke to life,
> I lay within the pliant, leafy branches,
> Which swayed upon the stem as sways a cradle,
> And thought I was new-born; I had no mother, –
> But that was nothing strange. I lay awhile
> Faint, weary, something soothed, till stung with thought
> As new-born things with hunger, I crept down
> And touched again the stony earth, and fled
> From all which had been, and could be no more,
> Setting Crag-Eyrie 'twixt my love and me.'

Mona, her fall broken by trees, decides to leave her past life behind her and live as a hermit in the Welsh countryside.

And now, having given Glân-Alarch two different versions of her suicide and its aftermath, Mona is reunited with Eurien. The battle has been won, Bronwen is dead, and Mona – now 'a virgin mother' – has saved the life of Eurien's son. Eurien now knows that this girl and the 'white maid who loomed so largely through the mist' (p. 242) are one and the same person. He now knows that she is:

> The same brave earth-clad soul,
> No fleshless spirit unassailable,
> But Mona as she was, – the highest dweller
> Upon the earth, but still on earth a dweller, –
> Rapt from their undiscerning, dull, brute gaze,
> And hidden somewhere in the heart of nature,
> Till they should hail her with the hearts of men; –
> Mona, his sister once, his slave, his plaything,
> Marked for his bride, then mourned for dead, then risen
> As rise the dead within the hearts that love them,
> And leading him still living, as the dead
> Will lead, for ever lead, the hearts that love them,
> The way of heaven, of glory, and of God.

Pfeiffer softens the transgressive impact of her suggestion that, like Jesus, Mona has 'risen / As rise the dead', by insinuating that Mona's supernatural appearances were more in the minds (or 'hearts') of her beholders than a reality. Glân-Alarch's thoughts return to Mona's suicide and the miracle of her survival, caught by the 'angel hands' of the trees. To Mother Nature, or the pagan goddess Gaia, Glân-Alarch offers up a paean of gratitude using gynocentric images of ripe fruitfulness, swelling sheaths and coming blossoms as signs of the promise of heaven (pp. 242–3):

> O Spreading arms, –
> Strong, supple arms, fruited, and many-fingered
> With autumn leafage, – ye that were upraised
> To Clogwyn Cromlech on that direful eve
> When Mona's heavy heart and light girl limbs
> Dropt from the sheer rock's crown, and were received
> Within you, I, Glân-Alarch, even I,
> Who love her only with an old man's love,
> Shall watch you when the season's change is swelling
> The sheaths of coming blossoms, to surprise
> Some sign of joy beyond your yearly wont,
> Some flowers that are as flowers of paradise,
> Some fruit that bursts with promise all divine,
> To credit you the ministers of heaven.

Pfeiffer again fuses Christian and pagan imagery in her creation of a heroine able to operate both as a human being and a disembodied spirit. Symbolising her Christ-like status, Eurien kneels and kisses the hem of Mona's robe in reverent joy (pp. 244–5):

> He sought her eyes, he clasped her trembling knees,
> She was again his sister, no immortal,
> His lost, his valiant Mona, whose great heart
> Was ever set to tasks that overbore
> The feebler flesh . . .
>   Eye to eye
> They held each other fast above the head
> Of sleeping innocence, while beating heart
> To beating heart answered through that soft bar.
> A moment still they trembled on the verge,
> Then lip to lip declined, and plunged their spirits
> Deep in the fathomless joy of the first kiss
> This twain had ever kissed as man and woman,
> A joy as wild as fire, more pure than snow,
> Unstained, keen, absolute, as flawless light.

As predicted by Mona, Glân-Alarch finds that he can sing again. He takes up his harp and sings a hymn of praise, hailing Prince Eurien, Mona, and the baby as 'the elected three / Charged with God's lightnings of love and of death' (p. 253). Mona takes her final journey back to Garth, where with Prince Eurien and his son she goes on to live a life of joy.

Emily Pfeiffer's blank-verse novel *Glân-Alarch* is extraordinary in many ways, not least in its creation of the character of Mona – an orphan, a waif, an outcast, a suicide, a hermit, a saint, a war-leader, a nature goddess, and a virgin mother – a young girl who is at once 'the highest dweller upon the earth' and 'a disembodied soul made free of the unlovely flesh'. This diverse array of attributes raises a series of questions. Is Mona a Christian or a pagan, or is she both at the same time? And how might Pfeiffer's depiction of Mona as the saviour of a hunted hare square with man's dominance over the natural world as set out in biblical text? Margot K. Louis makes this point:

> Close examination of the nineteenth-century scholarship and literature most influential in the creation of new attitudes to myth shows that deep religious impulses animated much of the work. Yet the spirituality that informed late Victorian mythography and mythopoeic poetry, in particular, was long unrecognized as such because it simply was not Christian.[18]

Louis goes on to observe the ways in which late-Victorian poets and mythographers 'engaged in an anguished and passionate debate that mediated the shift from various forms of Christianity to a far greater spiritual diversity'.[19] If this was the case, what was Pfeiffer's religious stance in this respect? In *Glân-Alarch* she combines the fighting qualities of King Arthur with the humanitarian qualities of St Melangell to create a heroine who, through a series of miracles, helps save the Welsh people from defeat at the hands of pagan Saxon invaders. But then she changes her story. Her heroine is not an emissary sent by God, after all. Mona is just a hermit living in a nearby valley – a kind of fertility goddess who becomes a virgin mother. Exploiting Victorian concerns about the Christian faith, Pfeiffer manipulates historical fact, myth, and legend to create a story that is both confusing and contradictory. Was Pfeiffer no longer a Christian? Or had she, in the process of integrating mythologies, found a spiritual way forward for emancipationist Christians?

It is the aim of the following chapter to address that question by focusing attention on Pfeiffer's mixed-genre work *The Rhyme of the Lady of the Rock, and How it Grew* (1884), which challenges women's spiritual marginalisation even further in a chilling double story of black magic, sacrifice, rape, and murder.

Notes

1. Emily Pfeiffer, *Glân-Alarch, His Silence and Song* (London: Henry S. King, 1877), pp. 7–8 (hereafter *Glân-Alarch*).

2. 'Mythopoeia', a term coined by J. R. R. Tolkien, is a genre which integrates real-world mythologies and archetypes into fiction. Tolkien was one of the twentieth-century Oxford Scholars who with C. S. Lewis and others formed the 'Inklings', a group inspired by nineteenth-century authors such as George Macdonald whose fairy tales and mythopoeic works such as *Phantastes* (1858) paved the way for later exponents of the genre – including Emily Pfeiffer.

3. *Glân-Alarch*, Preface, pp. vii–viii.

4. Laurie A. Finke and Martin B. Shichtman, *King Arthur and the Myth of History* (Gainsville, Florida: University Press of Florida, 2004), p. 1.

5. Ibid., p. 2.

6. Ibid., p. 60.

7. Catherine Brennan, 'Emily Jane Pfeiffer and the Dilemma of Progress', in *Angers, Fantasies and Ghostly Fears: Nineteenth-Century Women from Wales and English-language Poetry* (Cardiff: University of Wales Press, 2003), p. 160.

8. Ibid.

9. In her Preface Pfeiffer apologises for using English words and spelling in *Glân-Alarch*. During the nineteenth century both the English language and the Established Church were imposed upon the Welsh-speaking, and increasingly Nonconformist, Welsh people.

10. Finke and Shichtman, op. cit., p. 220.

11. The name 'Mona', derived from *Môn*, means 'mother of Wales'. Linked with fertility, the name first appeared in Gwynedd during the Roman era.

12. Louis, op. cit., Introduction, p. 1.

13. Ibid.

14. Ibid., p. 17.

15. As in 'From Out of the Night', where a young girl sacrifices her life for love. On her travels to Greece, described in *Flying Leaves from East to West* (1885), Pfeiffer was very much moved by the courage of the eponymous heroine of Sophocles' *Antigone* (c. 440 BC), where a woman who risks her life to perform a symbolic burial of her brother is captured and shut in a cave to die. While incarcerated, Antigone kills herself. Pfeiffer writes: 'The woman seems to rise to more than mortal height in the unequal contest: she is sublime, almost terrible, in her fearlessness; we are awed, we shrink before her in her unconquerable pride of duty . . . A word had done it, revealing the source of her strength . . . "Love and not hate is that whereof I know". That is Antigone' (pp. 63–4).

16. Arthur Findlay, *The Psychic Stream: The Source and Growth of the Christian Faith* (London: Psychic Press, 1939), p. 769.

17. Ibid.

18. Margot K. Louis, 'Gods and Mysteries: The Revival of Paganism and the Remaking of Mythography through the Nineteenth Century', *Victorian Studies* 47.3 (2005), 329–61 (p. 355).

19. Ibid.

CHAPTER FOUR

Re-Authorising the Scriptures

A RATHER DILAPIDATED VOLUME dated 1884, small crown 8vo, modestly priced at 3s.6d.; inside its worn cover, interspersed amongst the yellowing leaves of prose like pressed flowers, sit tiny clusters of verse. Though superficially unprepossessing, Emily Pfeiffer's experimental mixed-genre publication *The Rhyme of the Lady of the Rock, and How it Grew* (1884), based on the Scottish legend of Lady's Rock, is a small Victorian masterpiece – charming, complex and mysterious.[1] The speaker of the prose frame narrative, a late-Victorian poet touring the island of Mull with her husband, is inspired to write a Scottish folk-ballad about the island's famous legend. Sitting in the ruins of Duart Castle, listening to the ghostly whispers emanating from its walls, the poet intuits what she believes to be the truth about a crime that occurred in medieval times, subsequently using this information to create her own poetic reconstruction of the legend. Later her husband reads her folk-ballad to a small group of auditors consisting of their hostess, Miss Macorquodale; Archie Cumming, Miss Macorquodale's nephew; Maisie, her young maid; old Susan MacArthur (the last living proponent of the island's ancient folk-ballad tradition); and an itinerant Swiss pedlar, or 'gaberlunzie' man.

In addition to her poet's Scottish folk-ballad, *The Rhyme of the Lady of the Rock*, Pfeiffer includes a Victorian prose narrative which not only frames the folk-ballad at the beginning and end, but also frames each of the ballad's sections, or 'Fittes'. After each Fitte has been read aloud, members of the audience are free to express their views on what they have just heard in ways reminiscent of Chaucer's *Canterbury Tales* (c. 1387), which incorporated 'audience participation' to reflect the England of his day. Likewise Pfeiffer juxtaposes the medieval characters in her folk-ballad against the Victorian auditors in her frame narrative in order to expose and exploit sensitive issues of her day. The process of separating each section of a narrative with an interval of audience feedback seems to have the general effect of increasing the audience's desire to find out what is going to happen next. This trend can be seen in the anticipation of new instalments of novels published in serial form – novels such as those serialised by Charles Dickens. Pfeiffer, by fusing two genres and two different worlds of experience into a drama created and orchestrated by herself, shines a spotlight on the intersecting oppressions of gender and religion in nineteenth-century Britain. Owing to the structural complexity of *The Rhyme of the Lady of the Rock, and How it Grew*, however, I shall briefly summarise each section in sequence so that I can then go on to discuss specific issues raised by the work.

Frame Narrative

In her lengthy introductory frame narrative, the 'Poet' describes how she and her German husband Helmuth (presumably doubling for Emily Pfeiffer and her German husband Edward) are delayed by a violent storm which prevents them from crossing from Oban on the mainland to the Isle of Mull.[2] Eventually they get under way, their ferry passing the sinister ocean rock where, in medieval times, the young wife of the Chieftain of Mull had been left to die in a storm. Later the Poet sits alone in the ruins of Duart Castle where, distancing herself from the 'definitive' version of the legend of Lady's Rock, she constructs her own version. Eventually, after a number of embarrassing misunderstandings, the Poet and her husband find themselves comfortably ensconced in Miss Macorquodale's guesthouse. At the request of the islanders, the Poet's husband reads her version of the legend, which she has set out in the form of a Scottish folk-ballad, to the assembled group.

Fitte the First

Elizabeth Campbell is bartered to the tyrant Lachlan Maclean of Mull by her brother, regardless of the fact that she loves, and is loved by, one of her own Campbell clansmen. Before leaving the mainland, she vows to be true to the man she loves.

Frame Narrative

The Swiss pedlar finds fault with the Poet's reference to a nightingale in her ballad, since nightingales are unknown in Scotland. Then he finds fault with the poem's irregular metre, displaying his ignorance of the Scottish folk-ballad genre.

Fitte the Second

On her wedding night Elizabeth prays to the Virgin Mary. Hidden between her breasts she has a dagger disguised as a golden dragon in jewelled mail. She plans her defensive strategy. When Maclean enters her bower, she suggests that the marriage should remain a marriage in name only, but Maclean dismisses the idea. When she reveals her dagger to kill herself, however, he fears retaliation from the clan Argyle. Drunk as he is, he is prepared to defer his pleasure for one night.

Frame Narrative

This time the pedlar accuses the Poet of coarseness and immorality, predicting that the London critics will come down on her like a ton of bricks. Helmuth stands up for his wife and all the other auditors are supportive. The Poet is forced to admit, however, that the pedlar might be right, and that there was trouble in the wind. Yet she writes: 'If there was toll to pay in taking that path, I would pay it, bringing this small sacrifice to the cause of freedom, as many a woman in this generation has brought a greater' (p. 131).

Fitte the Third

Maclean fails to consummate his marriage, so he sublimates his lust by going out on bloody raids. Meanwhile, at Duart Castle, Elizabeth proves herself to be a hard-working and much beloved chatelaine who treats everyone, even Maclean, with the utmost respect and courtesy. Maclean is now reduced to pleading with her to be allowed into her bed, but she remains loyal to the man to whom she vowed to be true. Gradually Maclean's fantasies take a more sinister turn.

Frame Narrative

The pedlar, ignoring the Poet and rudely addressing her husband, continues to criticise the ballad, but Miss Macorquodale interjects: 'If the beautiful poem gives this gentleman no more to say . . . it is the better for those that would like to be hearing it speak for itself' (p. 140). The reading continues.

Fitte the Fourth

Eventually on one of his raids Maclean takes a lover whom he brings back to Mull in order to humiliate Elizabeth. But Elizabeth is unaffected by the arrival of Maclean's 'limmer' (or 'strumpet'), and so Maclean becomes even more frustrated. Meanwhile the 'limmer' wishes to topple Elizabeth and take her place as chatelaine of Duart Castle. She makes a wax effigy of Elizabeth which, by muttering black magic incantations over it, she turns into a fetish. Then she stabs it through the heart. She and Maclean together hatch an evil plan as Maclean repeatedly stabs the effigy.

Frame Narrative

The Swiss pedlar is now extremely agitated: he attacks women who want to emancipate themselves, stating that they cannot follow men 'into the clouds' (p. 147): men are better than women in every respect. Helmuth gallantly supports his wife as the pedlar continues to rail against her. The pedlar is upset that the story has no hero, and sympathises with Maclean because he has been deprived his marital rights just to spare Elizabeth's 'daintiness'. Everything is Elizabeth's fault. Outside the storm is raging. The pedlar takes to shouting over Helmuth's voice as he tries to read the ballad to the assembled group.

Fitte the Fifth

Maclean and his henchmen row Elizabeth to the rock. A storm is coming. Maclean rapes her and leaves her on the rock with the spring tide coming in and the storm in full spate. Soon the rock will be submerged. At first Elizabeth tries desperately to clamber into the departing shallop, but is roughly thrown back. She weeps for the loss of her virginity and asks the Virgin Mary to let her lover know that her heart was true. Miraculously her virginity is restored as the waves start to rise up her body. She shakes her spirit free, and lies washed as for the grave.

Frame Narrative

At some undisclosed point, during the recitation of Fitte the Fifth, the pedlar walks out into the storm. Now, with the meal to cook, only three auditors are left to hear the end of the ballad.

Fitte the Sixth

Two boats cross the sea from the Island of Mull to the mainland. The first boat to cross over is rowed by one of Maclean's blood-thirsty henchmen, a 'red-handed' murderer called Shamesh, and in his boat is the lifeless body of Elizabeth (p. 173). It transpires that after Elizabeth's rape Shamesh had 'sighted' her soul as it rose, and because he could not get rid of this 'sight' – and the sound of her cries ringing in his ears – he had decided to row all the way back from Duart Castle to the ocean rock in the storm to rescue Elizabeth. Then picking up her lifeless body he had rowed it – not back to Mull, but instead all the way across the Firth of Lorne in the storm to the Scottish mainland, depositing Elizabeth's lifeless body on the beach at Dunnolly Bay.

The second boat to leave Mull carries Maclean and a funeral cortège escorting the corpse-like wax effigy of Elizabeth. Meanwhile, however, Elizabeth has come back to life and been reunited with her true-love, telling her clan of Maclean's treachery. Soon afterwards, a grieving Maclean and his mourners arrive with what appears to be the dead body of Elizabeth. To Maclean's horror, Elizabeth appears before him and burns the effigy. Maclean leaves the castle as fast as he can, never to return. Elizabeth marries the man she loves.

Frame Narrative

At the end of the recitation, Miss Macorquodale finds she has over-boiled the potatoes; the old Sibyl, Susan MacArthur, has fallen asleep; Archie Cumming and Maisie are dreamy-eyed, but silent. Yet the Poet is not discouraged. She is satisfied that she has obeyed the impulse 'to plough, not the fields of earth, but the air' and she expresses the hope that by so doing she has not merited rebuke from 'the Lord of all harvests' (p. 184). Finally Maisie thrusts some white heather into the Poet's hand, and the Poet is heartened by the knowledge that it is with the young that the future lies.

The 'Poet'

It needs to be appreciated from the start that the Poet is not a real person, but rather a character created from the imagination of Emily Pfeiffer. Deployed as a stalking horse to protect Pfeiffer from the adverse criticism that she feared might follow publication of her boldly experimental mixed-genre work, Pfeiffer depicts the Poet as a modest, conciliatory, and self-deprecating wife. Read at face value, the Poet's docility seems exaggerated, but if, as I argue, the ballad conceals a transgressive emancipationist undertow, Pfeiffer's characterisation of her genteel Poet is fully justified. Pfeiffer hides behind her Poet speaker, making sure that it is she who expresses controversial religious ideas and receives criticism, and not her. Pfeiffer also emphasises the presence of a supportive husband to give her Poet (and thus herself) married respectability: a masculine voice of reason against which to juxtapose dissenting patriarchal voices. Then she creates the character of the offensive Swiss pedlar to channel critical attention both towards, and away from, her heretical subtext. Pfeiffer further protects herself from censure by couching her verse within a formal ballad structure and by camouflaging her subversive subtext against the patriarchal backdrop of chivalry.

Although Pfeiffer presents her Poet as unlike herself, there are similarities. Like Pfeiffer, the Poet is part Celt, and like Pfeiffer the Poet and her German husband are Victorians touring the Scottish Highlands in the final decades of the nineteenth century. Clearly Pfeiffer wants to be identified with her compliant Poet narrator who, anxious to please, acts out socially acceptable roles. Yet at the same time Pfeiffer uses the Poet's voice to comment on controversial issues relating to the spiritual emancipation of women. Thus the Poet's narrative voice combines elements of conformity and non-conformity, fantasy and reality, naïveté and authority, compliance and obstinacy.

These contradictory facets of the Poet's personality, revealed in the frame narrative and echoed in the folk-ballad, blur autobiographical and fictional elements to produce a sense of ambiguity. Pfeiffer constructs a pseudo-autobiographical frame narrative to provide a sense of respectability, authenticity, and credibility that she hopes will, by association, rub off on her transgressive double story as if, hiding behind her Poet doppelgänger, she herself intends to share in Elizabeth's sacrifice, suffering, and heavenly reward. For it is not just Elizabeth who suffers to save her clan in this work; Pfeiffer's Poet speaker also suffers to save her 'clan' – a 'clan' probably composed of emancipationists similar to Pfeiffer herself. The Poet uses the phallic power of her pen to reconstruct the island's legend, just as her heroine, Elizabeth, uses the phallic power of her dagger (with its dragon and chain mail) to retain her virginity and spiritual integrity. Both women must suffer for their audacity – one by literary, and the other by physical, rape.

Early on in the frame narrative, Pfeiffer's Poet speaker distances herself from the definitive version of the Legend of Lady's Rock as popularised by Joanna Baillie (1762–1851) in her play *The Family Legend* in 1810,[3] a play she asserts 'I had never read . . . it was among the many things which had left no trace in memory. I preferred going to the source . . . dealing with the original material for myself (p. 43). Baillie's play faithfully adheres to the definitive version of the legend told to her by the Hon. Mrs Damer in 1805 as 'a legend long preserved in the family of her maternal ancestors',[4] a version claimed to be 'authentic as delivered from age to age in ancient Gaelic songs; and it is likewise a tradition [passed] from generation to generation in the family of Argyll'.[5] In Baillie's text the crime occurs in the fifteenth century, and the victim is called Helen. The girl's father, a Campbell, sells Helen in marriage to Lachlan Maclean, the Chieftain of Mull, by whom she has a child. Maclean's kinsmen, however, reject the idea of a Campbell heir and leave Helen to drown on the rock. Fortunately Helen's cries are heard by fishermen and she is rescued.

The Poet's failure to recall this version of the legend is interesting, for Pfeiffer must surely have known about it, having toured Mull with her husband in the early 1880s. But there was surely more mileage for Pfeiffer's emancipationist vision in constructing her own version of legend starring a heroine of her own making – a Scottish heroine called Elizabeth, a woman proud to suffer to save her clan.

In the light of my analysis of such poems as 'The Crown of Song', 'Madonna Dūnya' and *Glân-Alarch, His Silence and Song*, where miracles punctuate the life-events of Pfeiffer's heroines, the parallels between Elizabeth Campbell's life and death and those of Jesus, as recorded in the New Testament, seem clear. Elizabeth, sacrificed to save her clan, is sent across the sea away from her home, betrayed, raped, and murdered – and yet she returns home again. These events, analogous to Jesus' life, sacrifice, betrayal, death, and ascent to heaven, support my contention that Pfeiffer's ballad should be read as a Christian allegory. In addition, I argue that the religious implications riding on the back of the Poet's rejection of the 'authorised' version of the legend of Lady's Rock in favour of her own version (eleven years before Elizabeth Cady Stanton published *The Woman's Bible* in 1895), suggests that Pfeiffer had already, albeit allegorically, rejected elements of the patriarchal version of the Christian myth in favour of a version consistent with her feminist values.[6]

After she arrives at Mull, the Poet scours the island in search of surviving proponents of the ancient Gaelic ballad tradition, eventually finding the island's very last repository of this dying tradition in the person of old Susan MacArthur, who says to the small group assembled in Miss Macorquodale's kitchen: 'It's a pity to be sure that ye'll no hae the Gaelic; it's in the Gaelic that the pick o' the songs is to be found.' The old woman then straightens herself upon her chair, 'And there arose in the place a thin thread of quavering sound, high and shrill in parts, at times utterly mournful, but not without variety of expression . . . To the surprise of my ignorance, old Susan was not reciting but singing' (pp. 86–7).

The Poet describes the scene as the old woman finishes her song: 'The Sibylline expression had departed from the old woman's countenance, and the rigidity from her frame; her mouth resumed its aimless working, and her figure its attitude of feeble maundering' (p. 87). Pfeiffer's Poet searches Mull and finds an old Sibyl – an ancient relic of the island's dying folk culture. Invited to visit Duart Farm, this ancient Sibyl sings snatches of long-forgotten songs and ballads. Sung in the Gaelic, the Poet cannot understand the old woman's language and has difficulty in trying to 'select some accordant notes from among the discords' (p. 88). Yet, after piecing together these remnants of the island's age-old oral tradition, the Poet feels sufficiently empowered to carry on the tradition herself. As self-appointed bard and 'singer', following in the footsteps of the old Sibyl (named after the pagan goddess vouchsafed gifts of prophecy by the gods), Pfeiffer's Poet breathes new life into the dying folk-ballad tradition. She writes her own version of the island's legend in the form of a Scottish folk-ballad and then asks her husband Helmuth to recite it to a group of islanders.

When Helmuth recites the Poet's folk-ballad to the small group of auditors, he is following an ancient tradition dating back to a time when the sole method of communication was by word-of-mouth. Later on, when ballads were first put into print, they naturally reflected the diversity of the original songs and stories told, or sung, to tribal groups. Messages woven into narratives had different meanings for different members of different clans, and variations were accepted as intrinsic features of this living genre. Yet, as Matthew Campbell explains, in the eighteenth century the poet James Macpherson (1736–96) tried to create a Scottish national identity by ironing out cultural and historical variations in ballads. This resulted in the 'authorised' version of what he deemed to be 'authentic' ballads. Standardisation led to the creation of a false, romanticised, 'synthetic' Scots that was incorporated into Walter Scott's *Minstrelsy of the Scottish Border* (1803). Scott, as self-appointed bard, transferred cultural authority from the oral tribal tradition to the 'educated' literary reader. But when the Scottish ballad became 'authorised', and then taken up by the educated male Saxon 'bard', it ceased to be a living genre, becoming instead a vehicle for nineteenth-century nostalgia and 'Celticism', as exemplified by 'bards' such as Scott. 'Much English Victorian poetry and criticism,' writes Campbell, 'borrows wholesale from the writing of the Celtic fringes of the UK'.[7] This synthetic Celtic mode (or 'Celticism') was subsequently adopted by Alfred, Lord Tennyson who, as poet laureate, wrote Romantic and post-Romantic poems about King Arthur and other mythical Celts who dwelt in transitory Celtic outposts, far removed from reality. He evoked a Celtic past that never really existed using a language that was never actually spoken and, like Keats before him and William Morris, Dante Gabriel Rossetti and others after him, he glorified chivalry.

Campbell draws attention to the fact that Matthew Arnold, in his lecture *On the Study of Celtic Literature* (Oxford lectures of 1865–6, published in 1867), felt that an understanding of Celtic culture would help fusion of the Union. Arnold felt that Macpherson's work, however inauthentic, added 'the stormy west to the romantic and Victorian vogue for sublime locations'.[8] Later, in his essay 'The Study of Poetry' (1880), Arnold, in a bid to rate poetry higher than history, sidelined 'provincial' accents in favour of the English accents of the south-east – the accents of power, law, and administration – refusing even to recognise Chaucer and Robert Burns as classic authors, as they lacked 'high style'. Not surprisingly, in this literary hot-house, Celtic poetry struggled for recognition while hybridity became a hallmark of Victorian Romantic poetry. For Arnold, a culturally complete and centralising modern United Kingdom was dependent on 'an intermarriage of the feminine Celt and the masculine Saxon'.[9]

The assignment of masculinity to a dominant ethnic group and femininity to a marginalised ethnic group epitomises patriarchal ascendancy – male over female, Saxon over Celt, received English over Gaelic brogue. Yet apart from gender, ethnicity, and language, patriarchal power also controlled religious and economic factors. Thus the contemporary masculine, Saxon, Protestant held political sway over the Celtic, feminine, Catholic. In the mid-nineteenth century, for example, there developed a view-point 'which associated the feminine, the Catholic, and the Celtic in opposition to what were characterized as the English, Protestant, "male" assumptions of political economy'.[10] The association of economically and spiritually marginalised groups with women, and economically and spiritually dominant groups with men, therefore, saw patriarchal power ascendant over gender, language, ethnicity, economic power, and religion. Thus men dominated all aspects of life with the result that in marginalised Scotland the 'feminine', often Catholic, Gaelic, culture, having been 'authorised' and 'authenticated', became rich pickings for male, Saxon, Protestant plunderers.

In ways similar to the Scottish ballad tradition, the Judaeo-Christian religion gave rise to variants which were reflected in the rich diversity of early textual records. Later, from a miscellany of these records, came the 'authorised' version of the Bible, the Revealed Word of God.[11] This exclusive canon of the New Testament of the Bible became 'authorised', thereby becoming a static vehicle for patriarchal authority, as Elisabeth Schüssler Fiorenza explains:

> [The] New Testament . . . [contributed to] the historical silencing and textual marginalization of women . . . The political goal of establishing the unified church as the consolidating power of the Roman Empire drove the exclusionary selection and canonization process . . . The

tandem notion of orthodoxy–heresy was developed in the second and third centuries. This drive for the 'orthodox' self-identity of the 'patristic' churches was motivated by political factors and had as an attendant outcome the identification of women's Ecclesiastical leadership as heresy.[12]

To challenge the authenticity of the Bible was to be regarded as a heretic, as Bishop Colenso of Natal (1814–83) discovered when he let it be known that the facts of the Pentateuch did not tally.[13] Other nineteenth-century men to challenge the Bible as the Revealed Word of God were David Friedrich Strauss whose publication *Das Leben Jesu* (1835) was translated from the German by Marian Evans (George Eliot) as *The Life of Jesus, Critically Examined* (1846) and later by the poet Mathilde Blind as *The Old Faith and the New: A Confession* (1873), and Ernest Renan in his *Vie de Jésus* (1863).[14] Renan, a French Catholic Hebrew scholar, came to believe that although the Gospels may be true in essence, they are embellished with miraculous folk-tales which are not. The possibility that the Bible was a human, and not a divine, construct also haunted Edward Pusey (1800–82), a founder of the Oxford movement.[15] On this subject, Jane Ellen Harrison (who was thirty-four years old when *The Rhyme of the Lady of the Rock* was published), writes:

> [Man] makes an idol, not in wood or stone, but in his mind . . .
> he bows down, calling it God. He then tells stories about the
> idol . . . If we ourselves are the makers of these tales, we call
> them theology; if others with whom we do not agree make
> them, we call them mythology.[16]

In terms of both transmission and authorisation, clear parallels exist between the Bible and the Scottish ballad culture.

In order to gauge Pfeiffer's possible reaction to the textual marginalisation of Christian women, I refer to an essay by Claudia Camp in which she quotes a question posed by Carolyn Osiek in 1985:[17]

> When women . . . in Christian communities become aware
> of their situation within a patriarchal religious institution
> and, moreover, when they recognize that the Bible is a major
> implement for maintaining the oppression of patriarchal
> structure, what are the ways in which they respond and adjust
> to that situation?[18]

Julie Melnyk describes the ways in which the social reformers Florence Nightingale (1820–1910) and Josephine Butler (1828–1906) dealt with this problem:

> [Florence] Nightingale's relative success in achieving empowerment . . . depended upon her unorthodox Christology, including her denial of the resurrection. This denial allowed her to evade the problem of where to locate Christ's power and authority: all power must be temporal.[19]

Like Nightingale, when Josephine Butler confronted the medical establishment, she exploited the identification of women with Christ-like suffering in order to gain the psychological and ideological upper hand. Unlike Nightingale, however, she saw the female Christ not as an individual woman but as a community of all women united in the same cause. Again, Melnyk explains:

> By collectivizing women's identification with the feminized Christ and by calling for apocalypse, Butler made the equivocal ideology of the suffering, Christ-like woman into a more empowering one, no longer requiring individual suffering.[20]

For Butler, group identification is seen as more powerful than individual identification with Christ and the suffering of one part of the group is seen as grounds for renewing the struggle to seek salvation for the whole group through a wholesale transformation of society.

Applying Osiek's question to Pfeiffer in terms of her response to her growing realisation (during the 1870s and 1880s) that the Bible helped to maintain women's oppression, it seems that Pfeiffer responded by infusing pagan elements into her religious poetry. In her allegorical *Rhyme of the Lady of the Rock*, Pfeiffer depicts her Poet double as a bard who inherits the ancient Scottish folk-ballad tradition from an old 'Sibyl' and in so doing revivifies an ancient matrilineal heritage. Thus the religious archetype that constitutes the divine standard of value consists of not one, but two, powerful female archetypes – the Poet and Elizabeth – that, fused together, become sufficiently powerful to overthrow their patriarchal oppressors.

In order to make her religious and feminist points, Pfeiffer creates two different sets of events, two different time-frames, two different genres, and two different narratives that impact upon two different heroines. The bartered bride of the medieval ballad is Elizabeth Campbell, and the Victorian Poet who bravely risks her reputation by re-constructing and broadcasting her transgressive version of the legend is a mirror-image of Elizabeth Campbell herself. The medieval heroine survives death because of her divine qualities; the Victorian heroine (who tells her story) is, by association, similarly imbued. In the form of a Christian allegory, Pfeiffer attempts to reclaim the temporal and spiritual power that a patriarchy denied Christian women in the Western tradition.

The Pedlar

Whereas Lachlan Maclean is the personification of evil in the medieval folk-ballad, Pfeiffer clearly intends the Swiss pedlar to be Maclean's nineteenth-century equivalent in the frame narrative. Depicted as a self-opinionated, pseudo-literary bigot, the Poet's description of the pedlar's appearance is correspondingly unattractive (pp. 83–4):

> [The stranger] was about forty-five . . . [with] iron-grey locks sparsely covering a large head very flat at the summit and wide at the sides; his eye . . . [which] seemed to invite the knocks of fate while it promised a sharp retort to them, gave me the fantastic notion in regard to him that he resembled a nail out of service.

The Poet proceeds to describe the pedlar's deprived upbringing (pp. 84–5):

> Driven from home by the tyranny of his father, a masterful, prosperous man [who] wanted to bend or to break all who fell under his hand to his own conditions . . . his violent cruelty had so wrought upon a more tender-spirited brother that the youth had put an end to his existence . . . As we listened . . . it was clear that this one at least of the tyrant's sons had inherited some of the stormy passions of the father.

A telling insight into the character of the pedlar, a man depicted by Pfeiffer's Poet as a tyrant similar to Maclean (albeit on a much smaller scale), occurs at the end of Fitte the First when he boasts about strangling a land-rail (or corncrake) one night on the moor. He brags (pp. 111–12):

> 'The land-rail is a weak, tricky bird; it will feign to be dead, thinking in that way to escape your malice; but it is easy

taken in with its own coin, for, like to deceivers in general, it is not less but more to be bamboozled than others. I laid myself flat like a dead weasel, and held in my breath, when the fellow whose call had been the sharpest came brushing my ear. If his summons was heard of a bride, it did not get him a wife; I put out my hand and took him – a bundle of feathers with a little limp body inside – but warm, and with a heart that you might count the beats of; but for that, he was a better actor than I. Anyway he kept me not from sleep the last half of that night.'

The pedlar scoffs at the land-rail's survival strategy of playing possum, flattering himself that he can see through the bird's deception. The power differential between the pedlar and the bird is vast, and yet the pedlar still feels the need to exercise power over this small creature – and so he throttles it. This anecdote has implications for women such as the Poet who, like the land-rail, adopt 'weak and tricky' strategies in order to survive in Victorian Britain. 'Tricky' women (like the Poet) who try to bamboozle men by pretending to be weak and helpless do not fool the pedlar. He is able to see right through their cunning. The pedlar, like the dead weasel he impersonates in order to out-manoeuvre a land-rail, fails to realise that he too 'like to deceivers in general . . . is more to be bamboozled than others'. For the 'weak and tricky' Poet's song continues Fitte after Fitte, hour after hour, until the pedlar cannot bear to listen to it any more and walks out into the storm.

After Fitte the Second, in which the events of Elizabeth Campbell's wedding night are related, the Swiss pedlar turns to address Helmuth: 'Your lady has set her pen to work on a perilous subject as addressed to your "Philister" English public' (p. 127). Horrified, the Poet sees her ballad through his crude perspective: 'My visions were scattered in a moment; like a jewelled window through which a bullet has passed, the hues of fancy grew dark and dull with the inlet of common day.' The Poet's husband rushes to her defence: 'The danger you speak of is beneath contempt . . . there is no work here for the literary scavenger but such as he may make for himself.' But the pedlar exclaims (pp. 128–31):

'I can make me a picture . . . of paragraphs in certain of your public prints wherein the critics will exalt themselves upon moral stilts, and will come down on [her] . . . The ladies who

choose to forsake the covered ways and to 'walk in the sun',
must take the chances that will befall them.'

At which the Poet considers the pedlar's words (p. 131):

> I had written of what, as a woman, I could feel as possibly no
> man could; if there was toll to pay in taking that path, I would
> pay it, bringing this small sacrifice to the cause of freedom,
> as many a woman in this generation has brought a greater. I
> looked up clear, ashamed of my momentary cowardice.

Distinct parallels exist between the Poet's statement highlighting
her willingness to suffer for her emancipationist cause, and Elizabeth
Campbell's statement: 'It has not been laid upon a man / But on me
to suffer and save the clan' (p. 104). Both women are proud to pay an
exacting toll for refusing to comply with patriarchal convention. Yet
Pfeiffer makes sure that it is a man, the Poet's husband Helmuth, who
directly opposes the pedlar's sexist criticism (p. 148):

> '[Women] have voices of different quality from ours – voices
> for singing no less than for speaking . . . Are there no notes,
> think you, that are beyond [man's] reach . . . ? Critics would
> do knightly service in the cause of music; but they follow
> each other with no more variety in their cry than the howling
> of wolves in a pack.'

Pfeiffer's depiction of the pedlar as a self-appointed critic, grandiloquent
but ignorant – a howling wolf in a wolf-pack – is a direct attack against
'un-knightly' nineteenth-century male reviewers of women's poetry.

Pfeiffer herself had good reason for fearing the destructive power
of this misogynistic breed and it seems rightly so, for even in 1884,
after publication of *The Rhyme of the Lady of the Rock, and How it
Grew*, a reviewer for the *Westminster Review*, writing anonymously,
compared Pfeiffer's frame narrative unfavourably with the work of the
male writer of his previous review:

> Even Mr. [H] does not subjoin to his passionate effusions
> a prose narrative of how he felt when he began to write, or
> what he had for dinner the day before; nor does he present
> us with a model audience consisting of several admirers and
> only one dissentient critic.[21]

For women poets, 'one dissentient critic' might seem more than enough if they are as destructive as the Swiss pedlar. But then the reviewer for the *Westminster Review* went on to criticise Pfeiffer's deployment of two genres within a single work, writing: 'Against this unnatural union of poetry and prose we protest altogether.'[22] And then, verbally wagging his finger, he made an extraordinary remark: 'Mrs. Pfeiffer should not have deprecated criticism.'[23] What criticism, one might ask, considering that the only person to be criticised in the whole publication is the Poet and the only critic is the pedlar? Clearly the reviewer for the *Westminster Review* had failed to understand that the Poet and the Swiss pedlar were fictional characters created by Pfeiffer and, as such, were not real. Had he bothered to read her work properly he would not have unwittingly identified himself with Pfeiffer's caricature of the pseudo-literary pedant. The reviewer's error reveals a subtextual camaraderie between the two men – real and fictional – based on a shared dislike of assertive women muscling in to what they considered to be their own theatre of command.

The pedlar, once more taking issue with the Poet (while ignoring the key sequence in Fitte the Fourth where Maclean's lover makes a wax fetish of Elizabeth), is upset because Elizabeth accepts Maclean's lover into her household (p. 152):

> 'The lawful wife . . . in this story that has no hero . . . is no model of Christian charity when she welcomes, and as you may say invites to sin, a maiden . . . in the hope to spare her own daintiness.'

The pedlar expresses concern that the story 'has no hero', but the truth is that he is upset because the story, written by a woman poet, has a virtuous, but proud, heroine. The pedlar is especially upset by Elizabeth's refusal to comply with the Christian model of marriage that legitimises sexual intercourse even in an arranged marriage. In *The Subjection of Women* (1869) John Stuart Mill, in collaboration with Harriet Taylor, compares marriage with slavery:

> Above all, a female slave has (in Christian countries) an admitted right . . . to refuse the last familiarity. Not so the wife: however brutal a tyrant she may unfortunately be chained to . . . he can claim from her and enforce the lowest degradation of a human being, that of being made the instrument of an animal function contrary to her inclinations.[24]

The pedlar, like Maclean, believes that a wife should submit to her husband's sexual demands whatever the circumstances, and sees Elizabeth's coldness as justification for Maclean's adultery. Hostile to the ballad, the pedlar's prejudice against women's emancipation starts to come to the surface and in his diatribe his choice of words suggests a theological subtext (p. 147):

> 'This metrical story [is] laid out . . . like the . . . child who builds his palace with toy bricks . . . The ladies – it is the same with them all – are tied down to time, to time and to space; their sphere is here and now; let them try to emancipate themselves from us others as they will, they may cast themselves from a height, but they will never follow us into the clouds.'

In his criticism the pedlar makes three biblical allusions in a sneering attack against women's emancipation. When he compares the ballad's metre with a child's toy palace, the metaphor seems contrived because children do not usually build palaces with their building bricks. Yet because 'palace' is a common biblical metaphor for heaven, it is possible that the pedlar is inferring that women are too childish to attain heaven. His subsequent remark, about women casting themselves from a height, is reminiscent of the sequence in Matthew 4:6, when the devil tells Jesus to cast himself down from a great height to prove that he is the Son of God. The pedlar's third comment, that women will never follow men 'into the clouds', again uses words similar to those in the Bible. In Acts 1:9 Christ 'was taken up; and a cloud received him out of their sight'. Pfeiffer herself uses 'clouds' as spiritual metaphors in her poetry, as exemplified by her sonnet, 'The Sting of Death', when she expresses doubts of ever attaining a heaven obscured by clouds:

> O Thou whom men affirm we cannot know,
>   It may be we may never see Thee nearer
>   Than in the clouds . . .
> We may not reach Thee through the void immense
>   Measured by sons . . .[25]

The frame narrative of *The Rhyme of the Lady of the Rock*, with its anxious Poet and misogynistic pedlar, draws attention away from the recognisable Christian tropes which punctuate the work. Yet, at the same time, the Poet pleads for freedom of literary expression (p. 131):

> Whoever aspires to wings must be free, free of the air, free of
> the sun . . . I had written of what, as a woman, I could feel as
> possibly no man could; if there was toll to pay in taking that
> path, I would pay it, bring this small sacrifice to the cause of
> freedom.

As metaphors, wings generally denote spirituality, but after Elizabeth
Barrett Browning described Aurora Leigh's aunt as living 'A sort of
cage-bird life', nineteenth-century women poets tended to conflate the
two images to represent women as spiritually caged – their wings (or
spirituality) weakened from captivity.[26] But here Pfeiffer's Poet's words
suggest that she has left the safety of the cage and is spreading her wings
– that is, she is risking her reputation by expressing her spirituality
freely as a woman. The nineteenth-century Poet and medieval Elizabeth
Campbell are united by their willingness to suffer to save their 'clans'.

By describing the pedlar's strangely theological reaction to the
knowledge that the Poet is an emancipationist, Pfeiffer makes her
allegorical points. The pedlar is a zealot, a Pharisee, like those who
tried to trick (and ultimately destroy) Jesus. The Poet has taken an
enormous literary risk, and now the pedlar has found her out and
taken it upon himself to destroy her reputation. In her ballad, the Poet
describes how Elizabeth's refusal to consummate her arranged marriage
sets into motion demonic forces which lead to her betrayal, rape, and
murder. Yet by constructing a Christian allegory in which Jesus, the
man, is emulated by Elizabeth, the woman, Pfeiffer also puts her own
reputation on the line.

Elizabeth

On her wedding night, Elizabeth Campbell reaches her turret chamber
and dismisses her bower maidens, asking them to pray for her (p. 118):

> She cast her garments one by one,
>   Alone as she stood there;
> She was to sight no summer flower
>   But a woman deadly fair,
> When forth she drew the golden comb
>   And loosed the golden hair
> Which sheathed her body to her knee, –
> A ringed and burnished panoply.

> Then, as a swimmer, with her arms
> The amber flood she spurned
> To either side, and in her hand
> She took a gem that burned –
> That rose and fell upon her heart
> As a thing that bore in its life a part.

At first glance it seems that the sexual symbolism implicit in this part of the ballad conforms to tradition: the archetypal long-haired medieval lady, weak but beautiful, yearns to be carried away by a powerful, chivalrous defender – an image distrusted by Aurora, in Elizabeth Barrett Browning's *Aurora Leigh*:

> I do distrust the poet who discerns
> No character of glory in his times,
> And trundles back his soul five hundred years,
> Past moat and drawbridge, into a castle-court.[27]

Pfeiffer has seemingly done exactly what Aurora eschews. Through her female Poet narrator she has trundled Elizabeth's soul back to the medieval turret of Duart Castle where she, a nobleman's daughter, her tresses shimmering around her (like the tresses of John Keats's 'Madeline', William Morris's 'Rapunzel' and Alfred Tennyson's 'Godiva', perhaps) waits naked to be ravished by the arch-enemy of her clan to whom she has been bartered by her brother.[28] How could Pfeiffer portray such brutality – she who had, in the Preface to her verse-novel, *Glân-Alarch, His Silence and Song* (1877), written the words: 'I have tried to penetrate the veil of chivalry' (p. vii)? While male poets such as Keats, Morris, and Tennyson might enjoy writing poems about heroic knights and long-haired women, in reality most medieval women were treated as chattels. And yet Pfeiffer seems to endorse a genre which emphasises masculine power and feminine weakness.

A closer look at Pfeiffer's description, however, contradicts this notion. Elizabeth's hair is a 'burnished panoply' – like shining armour – and she spurns it, suggesting that she does not value it (and in later decades many women chose to cut their hair short). As Elizabeth Campbell stands naked in her bower, her body exposed and proffered, she is the very image of vulnerability. All Maclean has to do is take her, and she cannot resist his power. But as she parts her hair (like a mermaid – or siren) she reveals a secret weapon concealed between her breasts (pp. 118–19):

'Twas a golden dragon in jewelled mail
    That lay betwixt breast and breast
Over that gentle lady's heart,
    Couched as a lance in rest;
And that cunning sample of goldsmith's work,
It was the handle of a dirk.

She drew it forth of its leathern sheath,
    And she felt its steely edge,
Then gave some drops of her quick young blood
    To its point, as if in pledge,
Ere she wound her hair in a silken thong,
And the dirk in that golden chain and strong.

There are interesting aspects to the way Pfeiffer presents this phallic appendage to Elizabeth's otherwise naked body. The dragon in jewelled mail evokes an image of a knight in armour, perhaps St George killing the dragon, that ancient symbol of evil, the word 'mail', flickering with its homophone 'male', suggesting invulnerability. So, although Elizabeth is naked and unprotected, her possession of the dragon in jewelled mail suggests that she has hidden within herself her own defensive weapon and, as she whets it and sheds her own blood, she pledges to defend her honour with her very life. Then she appends her symbol of phallic power, the dagger in its protective sheath, to her own body with her hair to symbolise her inviolacy.

At this point it is apparent that Elizabeth Campbell does not conform to the usual 'damsel-in-distress' stereotype. Although young and long-haired, soft and naked, she is taking arms in preparation for battle and possible death. She falls on her knees and prays to the Virgin Mary (p. 119):

She muttered many an Ave then,
    And told off many a bead,
Till her passion sealed her lips, for words
    But mocked so sore a need;
Then she stopped and listened beside the breeze,
And only waited upon her knees.

Then, re-clothed in her night attire, she stands up, 'white in her snowy pall, / A breathing image of death', and as she hears Maclean's footfall on the stair, she prays: 'As I am a child of the deep Argyle, / Souls of my fathers! Teach me wile' (p. 120). Elizabeth is not praying for a knight to come and rescue her, nor is she passively accepting her fate: she is praying for 'wile' – because she plans to outwit Maclean. 'It has not been laid upon any man,' Elizabeth had asserted, 'But on me to suffer and save the clan' (p. 104): words that, had Maclean heard them, should have filled him with forebodings of doom.

Maclean enters the bower and, as he moves towards her, Elizabeth immediately starts to advance her case. Their marriage is a political one brought about to bring peace between their two warring clans. Because of this the marriage should remain a marriage in name only, but Maclean laughs and dismisses her argument out of hand. Elizabeth puts forward her argument again (p. 122):

> 'You asked for a gage of my feudal chief,
>> But of me nor word nor smile;
> You sought but to better the strength you had
>> With the strength of the deep Argyle;
> You shall have your due and no more of me
> Than a contract's seal and warrantry.'

To which Maclean:

> He laughed in his beard: 'Ay, many have tried,
>> But all have tried in vain,
> To mete with a measure that was not his
>> The due of the red Maclean;
> Still with iron hand he has held his right,
> But never so close as he will this night.'

Elizabeth stands braced with her back to the wall as Maclean adds: 'By limb and life, / I'll use you as my wedded wife.' Proudly she replies (pp. 122–3):

> 'I am an earl's daughter', she said,
>> 'And my oath is worth a knight's,
> And I swear by the health of my mother's soul,
>> That the kiss which first alights
> On me as we two lie in bed,
> Shall have the force to strike me dead.'

Maclean responds by saying that in his castle he will do as he pleases, her oath is without substance; and Elizabeth shrinks against the granite wall as he tries to embrace her, but her 'flame-blue eyes' are clear. She brings out her dirk to kill herself, and even though Maclean is drunk he can see that she will carry out her threat (p. 124):

> Her hand bore hard on her heaving breast,
>   And he knew whereto it clung,
> And saw how her eyes on the turn of his,
>   Two deadly warders, hung;
> Then his caitiff soul succumbed to hers,
>   He let her go, and sprung
> Back with the cry of a ravening beast
> Baulked on the eve of a gory feast.

Maclean realises that if she kills herself the political advantage he has devised for himself will be lost and the Argyles will avenge themselves of Elizabeth's death. He decides to play a more crafty game: he will postpone his pleasures for one night and will take her tomorrow instead. Maclean falls into a drunken sleep, but Elizabeth keeps a lonely vigil, lying 'still and white'. But when the sun comes up, she steals out of the bridal chamber: 'And alone in face of the risen sun / She dared to weep; the day was won' (p. 126).

Elizabeth has put Maclean in a bind. Firstly she has argued that sexual intimacy is not part of the marriage contract and, secondly, she has promised to kill herself if he forces himself on her. At first, Pfeiffer's Poet depicts Elizabeth as passive, weak, and subject to male domination in line with the accepted male portrayal of womanhood of her day, and then she reverses the roles. The weak and vulnerable Elizabeth has a secret weapon and becomes chivalrous and powerful as she turns the tables on Maclean by refusing to let him have sex with her. Elizabeth's 'wile' proves to be the undoing of Maclean and, as he becomes ever more frustrated and confused, the balance of power within their marriage reverses. Maclean's continued failure to consummate the marriage strikes at the very heart of his self-esteem, upsetting the delicate edifice upon which his masculine pride rests. But every day that Elizabeth remains a virgin is a day of victory for her, and this gives her confidence and poise as she proves ever more attentive as Maclean's wife and beloved as chatelaine. Aurora Leigh may consider chivalrous men an outmoded subject for poetry, but she is happy for women to take over that mantle, as Aurora avers: 'The world's male chivalry has perished out, / But women are knights-errant to the last'.[29] Like St George swooping down to kill the dragon, so Elizabeth attacks male chauvinism with all the might of a knight-errant. Fighting for justice and freedom, Elizabeth risks her own life and spills her own blood to symbolise the great sacrifice she is ready to make to save her honour and her clan. This makes her not only a role-model but also an icon. Through her courage and wile, Elizabeth manages to stave off Maclean's advances not only on her wedding night but right up to the day he rapes her and leaves her to drown on the ocean rock.

Lachlan Maclean

Although he marries her for political reasons, Maclean expects Elizabeth to become his property. Elizabeth may be an earl's daughter but she is still now his chattel. Finding himself sexually thwarted, he calls on his tribesmen to accompany him on a series of bloody raids in an effort to to make Elizabeth warm to him (p. 137):

> And he thought: 'To this frost-bound maid of mine
> When I come red-handed in,
> Will the ice of her virgin pride break up . . .'

That Maclean thinks his marauds will excite Elizabeth demonstrates the crudeness of his mindset. Alfred Adler (1870–1937), the first psychoanalyst to use the term 'inferiority complex', classified men like Maclean as members of a 'ruling type [whose] striving for personal superiority and power is so intense they typically exploit or harm others to accomplish their goals'.[30] Maclean's cowardly assertion that Elizabeth is 'frost-bound' – or frigid – just because she does not want him is a response typical of men who feel compelled to boost their faltering pride by denigrating the women who reject them. He thinks of her as 'mine' even though she is patently not 'his', no doubt boasting about nights spent in marital ecstasy with his bride when, in reality, he has not even touched her. He is consumed with hurt pride, crazed with unrequited lust, and black-hearted with secret anger.

At first his frustration takes the form of love-sickness: 'Then he fell in longing by day and night / As the sick man longs for health' (p. 137). But as he becomes ever more frustrated, Elizabeth becomes ever more confident. He cannot even humiliate Elizabeth by bringing his lover back to the castle, and so his destructive urges take a more sinister turn (p. 142):

> And he who noted her morning face
> Grow clearer and yet more clear,
> Beheld her the only untamed thing
> Of all that came him near.

The real problem for Maclean is that Elizabeth's spiritual gifts lie outside his lowly orbit. Bringing her superior qualities to bear on her role as chatelaine, Elizabeth has earned the respect and affection of all, and this makes her powerful. He fears her superiority: 'He dreamed of tortures of rare device / As to give his passion ease' (p. 138). Like a spoiled child, he creates fantasies of hurting Elizabeth because, although he is ruthlessly able to bend everyone else to his will, she cannot be 'tamed'.

Her description as an 'untamed thing' brings two other 'untamed' women immediately to mind – Robert Browning's Pompilia (in *The Ring and the Book*) and Porphyria (in his dramatic monologue). Like Elizabeth, both of these women possess qualities that put them beyond the spiritual reach of Browning's famous murderers, Guido Franceschini and Porphyria's lover.[31] These men murder the women they cannot 'tame' because, like Maclean, their narcissism and despotic love of power is compensation for profound feelings of inferiority and worthlessness. The woman who cracks the defensive façade and exposes the narcissistic psychopath inside puts her life at risk.

The Wax Effigy

Maclean's unnamed lover, the 'limmer', described by the Poet as a 'climbing rose', is envious of Elizabeth, and is prepared to do anything to depose her, this chatelaine revered for her virtue. That Elizabeth is not threatened by her presence gives Maclean's ambitious lover the opportunity to advance her predatory plans. And so the climbing rose (pp. 141–4):

> it wound and wound,
> It was so soft and young,
> So lithe as the green shoots felt their way,
> But they hardened where they clung . . .

> And [the] limmer, striking deeper root,
>   Still darkly wound her way,
> For she hated, who only reigned at night,
>   The woman who ruled by day.

Maclean's sexually dominated lover is doubly envious of the power which, as chatelaine, Elizabeth wields by day, for her power extends only over Maclean at night. But, she thinks, 'He will set me by his side,' and this Maclean does; but because this manoeuvre does nothing to dampen Elizabeth's spirits she becomes desperate and resorts to black magic (p. 143). Gradually, with Maclean's power to support it, the 'climbing rose' becomes a parasite, squeezing the very life out of Elizabeth (p. 144):

> Dwindle and dwine in shade and shine,
> Till all be mine that now is thine.

This is the incantation of a woman consumed with envy of one more powerful than she. Having fashioned a life-size wax effigy of Elizabeth, Maclean's lover 'crooned the curse / As a troubled soul might pray' (p. 144). The curse and subsequent stabbing of the effigy by the 'double-hearted' lover are the outward manifestations of an inner compulsion to murder Elizabeth. But the wax-work of Elizabeth is no ordinary representation: for when the 'climbing rose' crooned incantations over it, it ceased to be just a wax-work and became a fetish – an instrument of evil. 'Fetishism,' explains the psychologist Arthur Rebus,

> connotes a kind of religious activity that emphasises the worship of inanimate objects believed to have magical or transcendent powers . . . [and is] often found in connection with *paraphilia* [which is] characterised by obtaining sexual arousal and satisfaction with some object, or some part of the body not directly erogenous.[32]

Such 'a made object', comments Eugene Bewkes, 'may by some appropriate rite be . . . endowed with indefinite power'.[33] The significance of the fetish, or fetich, is also described by Robert H. Lowie in the same publication: 'What confers upon the object its supernatural potency is solely the mysterious spell sung over it . . . Any object can become a "fetich" if only it has been ritualistically consecrated.'[34] Jane Harrison's description of 'eikonism' seems very similar to that of the fetish, but whereas some Christians construct icons of, say, the Virgin Mary in order to turn her from an abstraction into someone they can love and worship on a human scale, Maclean's lover constructs her icon of Elizabeth in order to change her from a real person into an object.[35] Once Elizabeth has been objectified, Maclean's lover is able to consecrate her lifeless image with magical powers.

Once Elizabeth's effigy has become a fetish, Maclean's lover stabs it through the heart. He scrutinises the waxen face (p. 145):

> 'My lady's face as she lives – not so;
> My lady's face', he said,
> 'Not as she lives to flout us two,
> But as – she might lie dead',
> Then each glanced up as in vague surprise,
> And shrunk at the light in the other's eyes.

Consumed with lust for the inanimate image of Elizabeth, Maclean frenziedly stabs the effigy with his weapon. Simulating the rape and murder to come, Maclean unconsciously acts out his fetishistic fantasies on the wax-work effigy, now an object of paraphilia.

The wax image looks like Elizabeth, but it is only a facsimile – a man-made object that can be moulded, manipulated, and abused. This image can be seen as a symbol of Elizabeth's false self – inanimate and powerless – emblematic of the kind of wife Maclean wanted to marry. The fetish looks real, but this is an illusion: it looks alive, but it is not. Inanimate, objectified, and fetishised, the image of Elizabeth symbolises spiritual death. As Elisabeth Bronfen, referring to the popularity of wax cadavers in eighteenth-century Florentine anatomical museums, writes:

> The fascination engendered when the wax cast depicts a feminine body has to do with the fact that the two enigmas of western culture, death and female sexuality, are here 'contained' in a way that exposes these two conditions to a sustained and indefinite view, but does so in such a way that the real threat of both . . . has been put under erasure.[36]

Maclean can now examine Elizabeth at leisure, knowing that both her sexuality and her existence are 'contained' and that she no longer poses a threat to him. The effigy pre-figures the fate of the real Elizabeth who, 'under erasure', is as good as dead.

The duality of two Elizabeths – one that is inanimate and fetishised, and one that is animated and virtuous – symbolises the double standards of chivalry, but in subversive reversal, like a mirror image of the traditional stereotype. The real Elizabeth has all the valour of a true knight, with her 'jewelled mail', but the wax image symbolises the old male stereotype of womanhood, the fetishised and idealised maiden, passive, victimised, and contained. The fetishised Elizabeth and the real Elizabeth are situated at opposite ends of the spiritual spectrum – one representing eternal death, and the other, eternal life.

Rape

In Fitte the Fifth, Pfeiffer uses the dramatic form of *The Lady of the Rock* to explore the issue of marital rape, a subject of repeated concern to nineteenth-century feminists. Mediating her ballad through intertextual codes imparted to readers in lines variously reminiscent of Alfred Tennyson, Robert Browning, John Keats, and Samuel Taylor Coleridge, Pfeiffer advances her religious allegory (p. 157):

> She left her wheel, she left her bower,
>> She followed the false Maclean,
> The piper piped them to the shore,
>> He piped a doleful strain:
> The pibroch of Macrimmon Mor:
> 'The way you go you'll come no more'.

The opening line of the stanza sounds familiar: 'She left her wheel, she left her bower' – the words an apparent echo of Tennyson's 'The Lady of Shalott': 'She left the web, she left the loom' (Part III, stanza 5). The audience at the recitation hearing these familiar words would perhaps – if only subliminally – fear the worst for Elizabeth. The Lady of Shalott dies: does Elizabeth die too? The accumulating alliteration of 'piper', 'piped', and 'pibroch' lend the lines a plaintive quality, adding to the feeling that something terrible is about to happen. The words of the pibroch spell out Elizabeth's fate: she will never return.

Pfeiffer builds up tension by opening the stanza with words familiar to her readers, thus adhering to the ethos of the traditional ballad while subtly manipulating their mood. Anapaests are used to increase the pace of the stanza, and the irregular beats heighten the drama relating to the blood-stained hands of Maclean and his 'grisly' crew in the following sestet. The lilting refrain-like musicality of the enjambed last two lines, describe how the wind and sea, personified, are in tune with Elizabeth's spirit as they sing and dance together (p. 157):

> The helm was ta'en of the red Maclean,
> The oars by Donald Dhu,
> And Shamesh, he of the bloody hands –
> And they were a grisly crew;
> But my lady's spirit rose bold and free
> 'Twixt the singing wind and the dancing sea.

Here Pfeiffer paints a gruesome picture by describing Maclean and his henchmen as 'a grisly crew', a description reminiscent both of the 'gaunt . . . crew' of crocodiles in Christina Rossetti's lyric poem 'My Dream' (1855)[37] and of Coleridge's formative ballad *The Rime of the Ancient Mariner*: 'They raised their limbs like lifeless tools – / We were a ghastly crew.'[38] With a nod to Sir Walter Scott, the Poet's 'grisly crew' consists of 'red' Maclean at the shallop's helm, with the bloody-handed Shamesh and Donald Dhu rowing.[39] The metaphor of 'bloody' hands is used here to warn listeners of impending murder as these evil men row Elizabeth out towards the sinister black rock.

White is the colour that Pfeiffer uses to depict Elizabeth, a passive victim trapped within a 'white' (or unconsummated) marriage. Readers would already be familiar with the fate of white Pompilia, the child-bride murdered by her husband in Browning's *The Ring and the Book*. Images of Elizabeth's purity, and allusions to the Virgin Mary in 'my lady's spirit', all add weight to Richard Cronin's observation that 'white may figure purity, but it may also figure death'.[40] Metaphors of whiteness and spiritual purity in this context cast the shadow of death over a scenario made still darker by Elizabeth's innocent exhilaration at the 'singing wind and the dancing sea', oblivious of the evil coming her way.

For as much as Elizabeth is 'white', so is Maclean 'red' throughout the ballad – red-bearded, red-handed and 'drunk with blood'. The importance of this colour as a metaphor is again emphasised by Cronin when he shows the way Keats uses the colour red in 'The Eve of St Agnes'; when Porphyro looks at Madeline's beauty 'his pained heart / Made purple riot', of which Cronin comments: 'Porphyro's redness is the colour of his lust'.[41] In similar vein, Maclean is also red with lust – blood-lust, power-lust, lust for Elizabeth – but, at last, after months of humiliation and frustration, Maclean is about to slake his lust and justify his 'red' image by tearing down Elizabeth's virginal defences (pp. 161–2):

> The red Maclean! None other than he,
> He has her in hand at last,
> And oh, ye smouldering fires of hell!
> This time he holds her fast;
> The teeth of the dragon beneath her vest
> Are buried deep in her bleeding breast.

The boat has been hauled ashore and Maclean has dragged Elizabeth on to the rock. He has her 'in hand' at last, and he holds her so roughly that 'The teeth of the dragon beneath her vest / Are buried deep in her bleeding breast'. This is the concealed dragon in jewelled mail, the device containing Elizabeth's dagger, her guarantee of safety from Maclean's lust. But now the deep penetration of the dragon's teeth into her flesh is a metaphorical portent of the rape to come. The device that had so far safeguarded her virginity has turned against her, and the bleeding it inflicts on her breast symbolises the imminent loss of her maidenhead. The dragon, emblematic of evil, is the personification of duplicity for, at the very moment when she most needs its protection, it seems to revert to type and take Maclean's part. Nothing can protect her now and this is the 'red' Maclean's moment of triumph.

The next stanza concerning Elizabeth's rape is a key part of the ballad; for this Pfeiffer uses an octet to convey what the audience fears are Elizabeth's last moments. The rhyme scheme is abcbbbdd, and the second, fourth, fifth, and sixth lines rhyme to emphasise the words 'alone', 'his own', 'down', and 'stone' – in a relentless, remorseless pressure, against which an abundance of anapaests conveys Elizabeth's futile struggle against Maclean's superior strength, bestriding her 'trampled shore'. This succession of anapaests ('shuddering lips', 'then he cast her down') grimly suggests the action of the rape itself – the rhythmical pulses in 'kisses he pressed and pressed' being particularly suggestive and dramatic. Hyphens and enjambment help to emphasise Elizabeth's rape as a continuous process, not just a moment in time, but a sustained and prolonged ordeal (p. 162):

> He stood with his bride on that trampled shore –
> They two, and they alone –
> With brackish kisses he pressed and pressed
> As one who would make his own
> Her shuddering lips; then he cast her down
> As a man might cast a stone,
> And the rock that was all that was left of the world
> Seemed sinking with that light weight so hurled.

The 'trampled shore' is a transferred epithet for Elizabeth's rape. Once 'trampled', it is spoiled; its value – like a girl's virginity – degraded in the eyes of men. The same word is used by Browning's Pompilia when she thinks of her mother, a prostitute, whom 'every beast' was wont to 'trample', and readers realise that Pompilia herself has been similarly 'trampled' by her husband. And here, Elizabeth has struggled so hard to retain her virginity in this political marriage, and all for nothing.

Pfeiffer describes Maclean, pressing brackish kisses on Elizabeth as one who would make her shuddering lips his own and, in this context, the word 'brackish' means water that is stagnant and foul. In this way, Pfeiffer presents a description of rape that is both repulsive and brutal. Then he cast her down as a man might cast a stone.

Adhering to her usual alternating tetrametric and trimetric metre, except in the last two lines which are tetrameters, Pfeiffer uses her profound technical ability to create the horror of a rape without actually mentioning it directly. The dramatic caesura in line five ('Her shuddering lips; then he cast her down / As a man might cast a stone') separates the rape from its aftermath, like the calm after the storm, as Maclean disposes of her abused body. The contrast between 'shuddering lips' and 'cast a stone' makes a greater impact because it is so understated, and the sudden displacement of Pfeiffer's reference to Maclean as 'a man' casting a stone shows how casual is his casting of Elizabeth to the ground. Although some other octets in *The Lady of the Rock* end with only three feet, here the last line is a tetrameter, although the four beats are irregular, the broken rhythm seeming to emphasise Elizabeth's broken condition: 'Seemed sink/ing with that / light weight / so hurled'. The irregular rhythm – iamb (or spondee), tribrach, spondee, iamb – and the break between the contradictory metaphors 'light' and 'weight' – highlight the paradoxical nature of a crime that means so much to the victim and so little to the perpetrator.

With irony Pfeiffer contrasts the lightness with which Maclean takes Elizabeth's virginity – her most treasured possession.

She means no more to him than that: a stone to be cast down. Elizabeth, a rape victim, has been defiled and cast down; for although she is the victim she is still, by the standards of the day, a 'fallen' woman and to be such is to fall short, to be an outcast – to be cast away. Hell awaits Elizabeth, for in the eyes of God there is no distinction between prostitution, rape, or marital rape: the victim is tainted with Eve's sin and cast down. In fact, men like the pedlar would feel sympathy towards Maclean for, although he is himself an adulterer, he is married to a 'cold' woman who, in their view, deserves to be raped.

Furthermore, Pfeiffer's words ('then he cast her down / As a man might cast a stone') would surely be recognised by the poet's auditors as an allusion to St John's Gospel where a woman taken in adultery is about to be stoned to death by angry men. Then Jesus says: 'He that is without sin among you, let him first cast a stone at her' (John 8:7). The men, ashamed as they confront their own sinfulness, leave one by one. When Jesus is alone with the woman he tells her that he does not condemn her, but says: 'Go, and sin no more' (John 8:11). In spite of this enlightened teaching, the same double standards that existed between men and women in Jesus' day still held sway both in medieval Scotland and in Victorian Britain. Elizabeth is no adulterer, she is just an innocent pawn caught up in a political arrangement between two tribal chieftains; yet because she is a woman she is guilty even in the eyes of her rapist, and cast down like a stone.

Miracles

Elizabeth, now powerless in Maclean's eyes, realises what her fate is to be. The 'rock' personifies a mental and physical state so laden with woe that it seems to be sinking under the weight of her fall. Maclean and his henchmen fight the surging waves to put to sea again but there is something white hanging on to the boat preventing it from getting afloat. It is Elizabeth crying out that she is not ready to die, but Maclean cruelly pushes her off. The fallen Elizabeth is left alone on the rock while the tide continues to rise (p. 163):

> My lady rose in the strength of her pride,
> She saw herself there alone –

> She rose and blest the sundering sea,
>> The islet was all her own;
> She rose and rose to its topmost ledge –
>> She made thereof a throne; –
> She cried: 'Maclean of Duart, farewell!
> We're parted now as heaven and hell!'

In this stanza, once again Elizabeth is referred to as 'my lady' and as she sits regally enthroned on the rock the spiritual innuendo is clear: Elizabeth is more than an earl's daughter – she is an icon whose virtue, virginity, and very life has been sacrificed for her clan. She is aware that the gulf between her virtue and Maclean's evil is as wide as heaven and hell, but her greatest distress comes from breaking the vow she made to her true-love (p. 164):

> Then she wept for ruth of her maiden truth;
>> 'O Love, have I waked for thee
> By day and night, but to face thee now
>> With this lothèd stain on me?
> Come, ocean, and with your bitter brine
> Sweeten these ravished lips of mine!'

Elizabeth asks the waves to repair the damage caused by her lost virginity and the heads of the westerly waves combine and turn south to form 'one vast, foaming mouth / That hungered for her evermore'. Then Elizabeth berates Love, calling it false for driving her trusting soul to such a wild death; and the waves continue to rise so that the rock is 'Scarce bigger now than a maiden's pall' (pp. 165–6). Then she cries and clings to the rock and asks the sea to take her life quickly, and the sea returns and 'kissed her clinging hands' (p. 165). Elizabeth is now about to be engulfed and she feels the current dragging her hair. Her hands cease to cling to the rock, 'She has shaken her spirit free' (p. 166):

> And still the breakers lift their crests,
>> 'O maiden Mary', she cries,
> 'Who will tell my lover my heart was true,
>> Who will right me in love's eyes?'
> But the hydra heads have come and gone,
> And in the face of death she still lives on.

The waves start to drag Elizabeth out to sea, yet one white wave returns to restore her body to its pre-rape, virginal condition. Then, like Coleridge's

Ancient Mariner, who blesses the water-snakes and is redeemed of his sin as the albatross falls from him, Elizabeth's body is cleansed to symbolise her spiritual redemption (p. 167):

> The battle-front of the daunted sea,
>   Though the waves still chop and churn,
> Is in forced retreat, the wavering tide
>   Has trembled long on the turn;
> Then one white wave came back and surged
> About her – and her lips were purged.
>
> And she lay there washed as for the grave
>   And purer than virgin snow,
> Her beauty seemed as a conquering power
>   In this its overthrow;
> Her eyes were blinded, choked her breath,
> Her ears were open gates of death.

Elizabeth's virginity has been miraculously restored and she is now purer and more beautiful than ever before. But she is dying, and her death also marks the end of Fitte the Fifth.

Elizabeth's death comes at the end of a series of trials which started with her bartering and ended with her rape and murder; yet alone on the rock, and in extremis, Elizabeth undergoes a spiritual metamorphosis. She blesses the sea and asks it to cleanse and purify her battered 'lips' which, obligingly, the sea does. Then she asks the sea to take her life quickly, and 'The mad sea melted at her commands, / Came back and kissed her clinging hands' (p. 165). Finally, having ceased to cling to the rock, and 'shaken her spirit free' (p. 166), she asks the Virgin Mary to make her right in her lover's eyes, and the waves stop climbing up the rock. It seems that Elizabeth, like Jesus (Mark 4:39), is able to control the waves, which not only respond to her 'commands' but surge around her body to purify her. Then Elizabeth asks the Virgin Mary to intercede on her behalf, and immediately the tide reaches its peak, and the waves start to turn back down the rock that would normally be submerged, with the exception of one final white wave which returns to purge Elizabeth's 'lips' once more.

'Shamesh', the name Pfeiffer chooses for the 'red-handed' accomplice to Elizabeth's murder in her poem, is an Old Testament name, synonymous with 'light' (for when celebrating the Chanukah

Festival of Lights, Jewish children light 'Shamesh' candles as part of their celebrations). Pfeiffer's Shamesh, however, is initially a violent man who – completely out of character – feels compelled to set out in the storm once more and row all the way back to the rock because he had seen Elizabeth's soul rise up, her cries still ringing in his ears (p. 173):

> He had sighted her soul when it rose and sued
> To his chief at her wild wide eyes;
> And the sea and the shore through the live-long night
> Had been ringing as with her cries;
> And they drew him whether he would or no
> With the cords of a man, and he had to go.
>
> So he found her there where the sea had laid
> And left her, but not a sound
> There breathed from her body, as mournfully
> The waves fell sobbing round;
> Then a stainless lily, alive or dead,
> He gathered her up in his hands, and fled.

Rowing Elizabeth's lifeless body back to the mainland, Shamesh lays 'that white lady' on the sand, her spiritual status conveyed in her description as a 'stainless lily'. White is the colour that Pfeiffer uses earlier in the ballad to depict Elizabeth as a virgin trapped in a 'white' marriage, spiritually pure and physically unsullied, but in this instance Richard Cronin's interpretation of the metaphor seems more appropriate – that whiteness figures death. The metaphor of the 'lily' – that funereal flower – is also used to create a sombre mood, the terms 'stainless' and 'lily' tautologically stressing both the importance of Elizabeth's miraculously restored virginity, and the carefully prepared analogy of Elizabeth's virgin state with that of the Virgin Mary, the Mother of God, whose traditional epithet is 'Lily'. As Roman Catholic authorities on Mariology explain: '[The Virgin Mary] is undoubtedly the loveliest flower that ever bloomed on the tree of humanity, and we are perfectly justified in addressing her as . . . "Spiritual Lily".'[42] Thus Pfeiffer seems to be implying that her saviour heroine, the virgin Elizabeth Campbell, is on a spiritual par with the Virgin Mary.

The Poet describes two shapes passing over the sobbing sea. The first is the boat in which Shamesh – like Charon crossing the Styx – rows Elizabeth's lifeless body back to her spiritual home. The second shape is devilish Maclean 'putting to sea / With the waxen shape that in hate of hell / His limmer had molten and made so well (p. 174).

Although Elizabeth is as white and lifeless as her wax effigy, as she lies on the warm sands at Dunolly Bay she takes her first gasping breath. Soon after she is reunited with her true-love and taken home to the Campbell stronghold. The Virgin Mary has answered Elizabeth's prayer and made her 'right in her lover's eyes' and, like a 'chartered ghost', Elizabeth 'glides' into her place in her brother's fortress and faces her kinsmen, 'for a wandering breath that told of her death / Had called them together in hall' (p. 174). There her kinsmen listen to her tale with mounting anger, and the women weep as they bear her away.

Maclean and his mourners duly arrive with the wax effigy of Elizabeth. Crying crocodile tears, Maclean tells Elizabeth's brother and clansmen that she has died from natural causes. But, dramatically, Elizabeth then appears with her brother and lover and confronts Maclean and his grieving entourage (p. 178):

> His lieges are thronging in hall and court,
>   And many bold men and true,
> But in view of that lady who dazzles their eyes
>   They cower and tremble too:
> 'Tis an unkenned sight, and a weird, to see
> A spirit stand clear of its own bodie.

The abject terror of Maclean's clansmen when they see Elizabeth alive in front of them but also lying dead in her casket is justified, for no doubt they are ignorant of Maclean's duplicity. But this stanza juxtaposes two 'Elizabeths' – the dead Elizabeth, symbolised by the wax effigy, and the living Elizabeth, a dazzling spirit standing clear of its body and shining with power (p. 179):

> She seized the brand, and tossed it alive
>   On the waxen shape where it lay,
> And the light full-fed leaped up to the roof,
>   And the night was a brighter day.
> Then the red Maclean, who, dabbled with gore,
> And abject with terror, fled out of the door,
> To his whilom lady became no more.

The wax effigy symbolises spiritual death, so by destroying it Elizabeth destroys the negative image of women as 'tamed' fetishised objects of patriarchal power. In terms of Pfeiffer's religious allegory, the burning of the false image surely suggests that Elizabeth has exchanged her earthly life for a spiritual life in heaven. Yet as a woman who, like Jesus, suffered and died to save her clan, Elizabeth's great sacrifice has implications for all women. All women now have the spiritual potential to attain heaven through the intercession of the Virgin Mary and Elizabeth (who from an allegorical point of view is the daughter of the Virgin Mary). No longer seen as sinful objects of male lust, women are free to live and love unrestrained by patriarchal law.

Reunited with her true-love, her virginity restored, Elizabeth is not, however, rewarded for her suffering by returning to heaven with an eternity of sermons, hymn-singing, and piety. Instead, Pfeiffer's Poet rewards her heroine with marriage, and an eternity of love and carnal passion.

Aftermath

After the recitation, the Poet observes that the 'pedant had gone his ways . . . accounting of the work but as a text for the display of his superior knowledge' (p. 183). The old Sibyl, Susan MacArthur, has fallen asleep, and Miss Macorquodale, suddenly remembering that she has a meal to cook, ejaculates: 'The potatoes iss boiled to just one smash . . . they will be no but good for the pigs.' The shy Highlanders Maisie and Archie Cumming seem to waken as from a dream, but say nothing to the Poet. Yet the Poet is happy (p. 184):

> I had had my moment of joy when on the window-seat in the old Castle the thoughts were seething within me; and yet a vocation upon which you have entered with the spirit of a votary means the sacrifice, the dedication at least, of your best energies to a single end, – the forsaking of all other objects and cleaving wholly to that one, – and where the inward impulse lacks the outward seal of success, the faith in a such a call must inevitable be wavering . . . But the impulse to plough, not the fields of earth, but the air, has been obeyed, and however unyielding it has proved, it were fatal to fall back.

The Poet describes herself as a visionary prepared to sacrifice all in the service of her vocation, even if her efforts fail to meet with success. With 'the spirit of a votary', the Poet sees her reconstruction of the legend of Lady's Rock as a spiritual mission that requires courage, dedication, and single-mindedness. The Poet is obeying a 'call' to plough not earthly, but spiritual, fields – an enterprise which, though unyielding, she feels compelled to pursue. To fall back now would prove fatal, and here Pfeiffer's Poet comes very close to admitting that her vocation is the spiritual emancipation of women. But there is a proviso: 'It may be hoped that the Lord of all harvests will not deem the work to which He has been thought to summon, to have merited rebuke' (p. 184).

At first, these words seem puzzling. In her allegory Pfeiffer has, through her Poet alter ego, created a goddess, a spiritual daughter of the Virgin Mary. Although the dying Elizabeth cries out, 'O Christ, must the whole dead world go down, / Entombed in the charnel deep?' (p. 165), it is not Christ's but the Virgin Mary's and Elizabeth's own spiritual power that saves Elizabeth, restores her virginity, and brings about her safe return to heaven. Yet now Pfeiffer's Poet is suggesting that she wrote the ballad, broadcast it at great personal risk, and suffered the pedlar's destructive criticism on behalf of a masculine deity who might 'rebuke' her for misinterpreting his message. Pfeiffer's deliberate misquotation, 'Lord of all harvests', is derived from Matthew 9:37–8, where Jesus says to his disciples: 'The harvest truly is plenteous, but the labourers are few; Pray ye therefore the Lord of the harvest, that he will send forth labourers into his harvest'. Pfeiffer's replacement of 'the' with 'all' could have been deliberate – possibly because 'harvest' has gynocentric connotations relating to harvest moons, seasonal cycles, fruitfulness, and pagan fertility rites, so Pfeiffer's reference to a 'Lord of all harvests' could be an exhortation for female readers to disseminate the good news about Elizabeth's resurrection and 'homecoming'. Pfeiffer may be asking women 'labourers' to help bring in a spiritual harvest for all virtuous souls, regardless of gender.

In her mixed-genre allegory, Pfeiffer presents a view of Christianity disengaged from patriarchal ecclesiastical institutions and doctrines. Risking charges of heresy, Pfeiffer courageously broadcasts her spiritual message. Picking her way carefully between allusions to a pagan matrilineal heritage on one hand, and the patriarchal power of theological dogmatism on the other, Pfeiffer constructs a religious text in which women are spiritually powerful and worthy of heaven.

Her mixed-genre work boasts several goddesses – the Virgin Mary, Elizabeth Campbell, the Poet myth-maker – and the creator of both the Poet and Elizabeth Campbell, Emily Pfeiffer herself. Offering women a means for resolving the problem of being both feminists and Christians, Pfeiffer successfully fuses gynocentric pagan and androcentric religious elements together into a *single* ideology.

Notes

1. Emily Pfeiffer, *The Rhyme of the Lady of the Rock, and How it Grew* (London: Kegan Paul, Trench, 1884).

2. To differentiate between the two poets – real and fictional – I refer to the fictional 'Poet' with an initial capital from now on.

3. Joanna Baillie, *Family Legend: Tragedy*, 2nd edn (Edinburgh: John Ballentine, 1810).

4. Ibid., p. 5.

5. Ibid., p. 6.

6. Twenty-first-century feminist theologians such as Rosemary Radford Ruether and Elisabeth Schüssler Fiorenza acknowledge their debt to Elizabeth Cady Stanton, who they see as the 'foremother' of feminist theology. Stanton's publication *The Woman's Bible* is considered to be a key precursor of modern-day feminist reconstructionist theology.

7. Matthew Campbell, 'Poetry in the Four Nations', in *Companion to Victorian Poetry*, ed. Richard Cronin, Alison Chapman, and Anthony Harrison (Oxford: Blackwell, 2002), p. 442.

8. Ibid., p. 332.

9. Ibid., p. 446.

10. Colin Matthew, ed., *Nineteenth Century: British Isles; 1815–1901* (Oxford: Oxford University Press, 2000), p. 197.

11. This excluded 'The Gospel of Mary', believed to have been written by Mary Magdalene.

12. Elisabeth Schüssler Fiorenza, ed., 'Transgressing Canonical Boundaries', *Searching the Scriptures: Feminist Commentary*, 2 vols (New York: Herder & Herder, 1994), 2, 5–6.

13. A. N. Wilson, *God's Funeral* (London: John Murray, 1999), pp. 108–9.

14. Ibid., pp. 135–7.

15. Ibid., p. 111.

16. Harrison, op. cit., p. 197.

17. Claudia V. Camp, 'Feminist Theological Hermeneutics: Canon and Christian Identity', in *Searching the Scriptures: Feminist Introduction*, ed. Elisabeth Schüssler Fiorenza (London: SCM Press, 1994), pp. 156–8.

18. Carolyn Osiek, 'The Feminist and the Bible: Hermeneutical Alternatives', in *Feminist Perspectives on Biblical Scholarship*, ed. A. Y. Collins (Chico, CA: Scholars Press, 1985), p. 97.

19. Julie Melnyk, ' "Mighty Victims": Women Writers and the Feminization of Christ', *Victorian Literature and Culture* 31 (2003), 131–57 (p. 131).

20. Ibid., p. 151.

21. *Westminster Review*, 66, p. 297.

22. Ibid.

23. Ibid.

24. J. S. Mill, *The Subjection of Women* (London: Penguin, 2006), p. 166.

25. Emily Pfeiffer, *Poems*, op. cit., p. 142 (lines 1–3, 9–10).

26. Elizabeth Barrett Browning, *Poetical Works*, op. cit., p. 379.

27. *Aurora Leigh and Other Poems*, eds John Robert Glorney Bolton and Julia Bolton Holloway (Harmondsworth, Middlesex, 1995), p. 143 (lines 188–91).

28. William Morris, 'Rapunzel', in *The Defence of Guenevere and Other Poems* (London: Bell & Daldy, 1858), pp. 60–2; Alfred Tennyson, 'Godiva', in *Poems 1830–1858* (London: Grant Richards, 1903), p. 180; John Keats, *Poems* (London: J. M. Dent, 1906), p. 122.

29. Elizabeth Barrett Browning, *Poetical Works*, op. cit., p. 490.

30. Richard Ryckman, *Theories of Personality* (Pacific Grove, California: Brooks/Cole, 1989), p. 108.

31. Robert Browning, *The Ring and the Book* [1868–9] (London: J. M. Dent, 1911), p. 25; 'Porphyria's Lover [c.1835], *Selected Poetry*, ed. Daniel Karlin (London: Penguin, 1989), p 17.

32. Arthur S. Rebus, *Penguin Dictionary of Psychology* (London: Penguin, 1988), p. 273. Examples of *paraphilia* in Victorian verse include: the nose in 'The Dong with a Luminous Nose' by Edward Lear (1877); the bones in William Morris's poem 'Concerning Geffray Teste Noire' (1858); and the arms and hands in Arthur Munby's poem 'The Serving Maid' (1865).

33. Eugene Garrett Bewkes, *Experience, Reason and Faith: A Survey in Philosophy and Religion* (London: Harper & Brothers Publishers, 1940), p. 12.

34. Ibid.

35. Harrison, *Alpha and Omega*, op. cit., p. 202.

36. Elisabeth Bronfen, *Over Her Dead Body*, op. cit., p. 99.

37. Christina Rossetti, *Complete Poems*, op. cit.,pp. 33–4.

38. Samuel Taylor Coleridge, *Poetical Works*, ed. E. H. Coleridge (Oxford Univeristy Press: Oxford, 1980), p. 200.

39. Walter Scott, 'Gathering Song of Donald Dhu' [1796], in *Poems Every Child Should Know*, ed. Mary Burt (New York: Grosset & Dunlap, 1904), pp. 126–7. Donald Dhu, imprisoned for forty years by his Campbell grandfather, would surely relish the chance to harm Elizabeth.

40. Richard Cronin, *Colour and Experience in Nineteenth-Century Poetry* (Basingstoke: The Macmillan Press Ltd., 1988), p. 39.

41. Ibid., p. 75.

42. Pohle and Preuss, op. cit., p. 21.

Conclusion

Victorian women's religious poetry used to be recognised by its close adherence to conventions from which little deviation was permitted; and because, in general, Emily Pfeiffer's poetry failed to conform to these conventions she was not considered to be a religious poet. Some of her religious poems included secular material, often with polemical and emancipationist subtexts. Some of her religious poems alluded to different belief-systems, such as paganism and the occult. Thus, though I press my case that Pfeiffer's poetry deserves a place in the canon of Victorian women's religious poetry, most of her religious poems fail to conform to conventions that used to represent the canon. Fortunately, today, the conventions of the past have been replaced by more realistic criteria for what constitutes a religious poem. Today Pfeiffer can be recognised for what she was – a profoundly original and creative religious poet.

Emily Pfeiffer cajoled, preached, adopted sage discourse, appropriated the role of the *Vates* Prophet, entered the masculine world, and put her reputation at risk – all with the express purpose of promulgating her emancipationist vision as widely as possible. It was of vital importance to her that her voice should be heard, because she had embarked on a quest to defend women from patriarchal power – power that she felt deprived women of equality in education, employment, marriage, and religion. Each of these inequalities, both separately and together, she saw as fetters binding women's souls, preventing them from attaining heaven. As she grew older, Pfeiffer became ever more forthright in promoting her feminist cause, relentlessly pursuing her mission to combat ecclesiastical misogyny, her aim being to reinstate women to their rightful place within the Christian religion.

A versatile and prolific poet, Pfeiffer bent her exceptional talents to the task of disseminating her controversial agenda in an outspoken –

yet often encoded and subversive – manner. Defending Christianity against science, Pfeiffer adopted a scientific argument to present women as better equipped to evolve spiritually than men. Linked with Jesus because they share with him the stigma of pain and suffering, the women she depicts will likewise be resurrected and will join Him in heaven. Comparing the sacrifices made by a 'fallen' woman to the sacrifices made by Jesus, Pfeiffer depicts a young woman as spiritually superior to her lover who, following his betrayal of her, is free to marry in a misogynistic Church.

To varying degrees, Pfeiffer's heroines display supernatural qualities similar to those manifested by Jesus. The biblical story of Jesus' immanence as a Saviour God, the supernatural occurrences that were witnessed during his life and after his death, and the mysteries surrounding his ascension into heaven, are all mirrored by Pfeiffer in a variety of ways, sometimes in the form of allegory, but always within the overall framework of her Christian faith. It is important to note, however, that Pfeiffer never seeks to replace Jesus with a female deity, but rather constantly strives to counterbalance theological doctrine with a more spiritual approach to religion. By introducing heroines with supernatural powers into her poetic works, Pfeiffer is validating Jesus' supernatural powers while, at the same time, writing women into the Christian myth. Clearly her aim is to confront priests and ecclesiastical institutions with the power of Jesus, the man. Jane Harrison makes the point:

> We have confused theology – a rational thing that can be intellectually defined, though it must never be morally imposed – with religion, an external reaction towards the unknown, the hidden spring of our physical, spiritual life.

Pushing herself to imagine a religion where women are recognised as spiritually equal to men both on earth and in heaven, Pfeiffer finds it necessary to replace patriarchal creeds and doctrines with an older, matrilineal tradition. She infuses pagan elements into her verse in a bid to imagine a heaven where feminine souls can flourish free from the institutionalised ecclesiastical misogyny of the Western tradition. She anticipates aspects of feminist theology, and imagines a form of worship that is currently being adopted by feminists in increasing numbers.

CONCLUSION

Today, in the twenty-first century, it is coming to be understood that during the Victorian period conflict between the demands of Christianity and the demands of other ideologies was rife and that this should be properly reflected in evaluations of Victorian religious poetry. Using her exceptional poetic gifts to depict religious women as equal to, or even superior to, men – both on a natural and a supernatural level – Emily Pfeiffer can now be recognised as a courageous religious pioneer and spiritual emancipationist.

Bibliography

PRIMARY SOURCES

The Anglo-Saxon Chronicle: The Chronicle of Florence of Worcester, ed. Rev. Joseph Stevenson (London: Seeleys, 1853)

The Letters of Matthew Arnold, ed. Cecil Y. Lang, 6 vols (Charlottesville: University Press of Virginia, 2000)

Baillie, Joanna, *Family Legend: A Tragedy*, 2nd edn (Edinburgh: John Ballantine, 1810)

Barrett Browning, Elizabeth, *Poetical Works* (London: Henry Frowde, 1904)

Blind, Mathilde, *Dramas in Miniature* (London: Chatto & Windus), 1891

——, *Songs and Sonnets* (London: Chatto & Windus, 1893)

Book of Common Prayer, and administration of The Sacraments, and other Rites and Ceremonies of the United Church of England and Ireland (London: G. Eyre and A. Spottiswoode, 1844)

Browning, Robert, *The Ring and the Book* [1868–9] (London: J. M. Dent, 1911)

——, *Selected Poetry*, ed. Daniel Karlin (London: Penguin, 1989)

Carlyle, Thomas, *On Heroes, Hero-Worship and the Heroic in History* (London: George Routledge, 1841)

Carroll, Lewis, *Phantasmagoria and Other Poems* (London: Macmillan & Co., 1869)

Darwin, Charles, *On the Origin of Species by Means of Natural Selection* [1859] (Oxford: Oxford University Press, 1996)

——, *The Descent of Man and Selection in Relation to Sex*, 2 vols (London: John Murray, 1871)

——, The Darwin Correspondence Project, University of Cambridge (2007—): <darwinproject.ac.uk/darwins-letters>

Frost, Maurice, ed., *Historical Companion to Hymns Ancient & Modern*, rev. edn (William Clowes & Sons, Limited, 1962)

Gosse, Edmund, 'Critical Responses', in *Victorian Women Poets 1830–1901: An Anthology*, ed. Jennifer Breen (London: Everyman, 1994)

Greenough, Sarah Dana, *Mary Magdalene and Other Poems* (London: Chapman and Hall Limited, 1887)

Greenwell, Dora, *Carmina Crucis* (London: Bell & Daldy, 1869)

Hall Caine, Thomas, ed., *Sonnets of Three Centuries: Selection* (London: Elliot Stock, 1882)

Harrison, Jane Ellen, *Alpha and Omega* (London: Sidgwick & Jackson Ltd, 1915)

Havergal, Frances, *Ministry of Song* (London: Christian Book Society, 1872)

The Poetical Works of Mrs. Felicia Hemans, ed. William Michael Rossetti, (London: William Collins, n.d. [1873])

Hickey, E. H., *A Sculptor and Other Poems* (London: Kegan Paul, Trench & Co., 1881)

Hymnal Companion to the Book of Common Prayer, with Accompanying Tunes (London: Sampson Low, 1879)

Hymns Ancient and Modern for use in the Services of the Church with Accompanying Tunes, rev. ed. W. H. Monk and C. Steggall (London: William Clowes, 1906)

Jameson, Mrs Anna, *Legends of the Madonna as Represented in the Fine Arts* [1852] (London: Longmans, Green, and Co., 1890)

——, *History of our Lord as Exemplified in the Works of Art with that of His Types; St. John the Baptist and other persons of the Old and New Testament*, 3 vols (London: Longman, Green and Co., 1892)

Keble, John, *The Christian Year: Thoughts in Verse for the Sundays and Holydays Throughout the Year*, 2 vols (Oxford: J. Parker, 1827)

——, 'Tract No. 89. On the Mysticism Attributed to the Early Fathers of the Church', *Tracts for the Times by Members of the University of Oxford, 1838–41*, 6 vols (London: J. G. F. and J. Rivington, 1840–41)

——, *Lectures on Poetry 1832–1841*, trans. by Edward Kershaw Francis, 2 vols (Oxford: Clarendon Press, 1912)

Levy, Amy, *A Minor Poet and Other Verse* (London: T. Fisher Unwin, 1884)

Lewes, G. H., 'On the Dread and Dislike of Science', *Fortnightly Review* 23 (1878)

Lewins, Robert, 'Humanism versus Theism, or Solipsism (Egoism) = Atheism', *Tracts 1877–1879* (London: Freethought Publishing Company, 1887)

Lindsay, Lady Caroline, *Lyrics and Other Poems* (London: Kegan Paul, Trench, Trubner & Co. Ltd., 1890)

MacDonald, George, *Princess and the Goblin* [1872] (London: Puffin, 1973)

——, *Phantastes, Faerie Romance* [1858] (London: Azure, 2002)

Meredith, George, *Modern Love, and Poems of the English Roadside, with Poems and Ballads* (London: Chapman & Hall, 1862)

Meynell, Alice, *Poems*, 6th edn (London: John Lane, 1898)

Mill, John Stuart, *On Liberty and The Subjection of Women*, ed. Alan Ryan (London: Penguin Books, 2006)

Morris, William, *Defence of Guenevere, and Other Poems* (London: Bell and Daldy, 1858)

——, *Complete Poetical Works* (London: Bickers & Son, 1894)

——, *Early Romances in Prose and Verse*, ed. Peter Faulkner (London: J. M. Dent & Sons, 1973)

Moses, W. S., *Higher Aspects of Spiritualism* (London: E. W. Allen & Co., 1880)

Florence Nightingale's Spiritual Journey: Biblical Annotations, Sermons and Journal Notes, ed. Lynn McDonald, 2 vols (Waterloo, Ontario: Wilfred Laurier University Press, 2001)

Norton, Caroline, 'Stevenson, Pearce' and 'A Plain Letter to the Chancellor on the Infant Custody Bill', in *Miscellaneous Law Tracts* (London: James Ridgway, 1839)

——, *English Laws for Women in The Nineteenth Century* (London, 1854)

Page, H. A., 'Religious Poetry and Scientific Criticism', *Contemporary Review* 12 (1869)

Pattison, Mark, *Memoirs* (London: Macmillan, 1885)

Pfeiffer, Emily [Emily Jane Davis], *Holly-Branch: An Album for 1843* (London: John Ollivier, 1842)

——, *Valisneria, or A Midsummer Day's Dream: A Tale in Prose* (London: Longman, Brown, Green, 1857)

——, *Margaret; or, The Motherless: A Poem* (London: Hurst & Blackett, 1861)

——, *Gerard's Monument and Other Poems* (London: C. Kegan Paul, 1873)

——, *Poems* (London: Strahan & Co, 1876)

——, *Glân-Alarch, His Silence and Song* (London: Henry S. King, 1877)

——, 'Madonna Dūnya', *Contemporary Review* 31 (1877–8)

——, 'Studies from the Antique' [Sonnets: 'Kassandra 1, 2'; 'Klytemnestra 1, 2'], *Contemporary Review* 32 (1878)

——, *Quarterman's Grace and Other Poems* (London: Kegan Paul, 1879)

——, 'The Pillar of Praise', *Contemporary Review* 37 (1880)

——, *Sonnets and Songs* (London: Kegan Paul, Trench, 1880)

——, 'Woman's Claim', *Contemporary Review* 39 (1881)

——, 'The Pilgrimage to Kevlaar' [translation from Heine], *Contemporary Review* 42 (1882)

——, *Under the Aspens* (London: Kegan Paul, Trench, 1882)

——, 'A Rhyme for a Time', *Contemporary Review* 45 (1884)

——, *The Rhyme of the Lady of the Rock, and How It Grew* (London: Kegan Paul, Trench, 1884)

——, *Flying Leaves from East and West* (London: Field and Tuer, 1885)

——, 'The Suffrage for Women', *Contemporary Review* 47 (1885)

——, *Sonnets*, rev. edn (London: Field & Tuer, 1886)

——, *Women and Work: An Essay Treating on the relation to Health and Physical Development of the Higher Education of Girls, and the Intellectual or More Systematised Effort of Women* (London: Trübner & Co., 1888)

——, *Flowers of the Night* (London: Trübner & Co, 1889)

Pohle, The Rt. Rev. Msgr. Joseph, and Arthur Preuss, *Mariology: A Dogmatic Treatise on the Blessed Virgin Mary, Mother of God, with an appendix on the Worship of the Saints, Relics, and Images*, 2nd rev. edn (London: B. Herder, 1916)

Procter, Adelaide A., *Legends and Lyrics* (London: Bell and Daldy, 1866)

——, *Complete Works* (London: George Bell, 1905)

Pusey, Rev. E. B., DD, *Letter to His Grace the Archbishop of Canterbury on some circumstances connected with the Present Crisis in the English Church* (Oxford: John Henry Parker, 1842)

Rives, Amélie [Princess Troubetzkoy], 'The Wonderful Child', in *As the Wind Blew* (London: Hurst & Blackett, Ltd, 1922)

Robertson, Eric S., *English Poetesses: A Series of Critical Biographies* (London: Cassell & Co. Ltd., 1883)

Robinson, A. Mary F. [Madame Duclaux], *Collected Poems, Lyrical and Narrative* (London: T. Fisher Unwin, 1901)

Rossetti, Christina, *Complete Poems*, ed. R. W. Crump (London: Penguin Books, 2005)

Rossetti, Dante Gabriel, 'Sonnets and Songs, towards a Work to be called The House of Life', in *Poems & Translations, 1850–1870* (London: Oxford University Press, 1926)

——, *The House of Life*, with introduction and notes by Paull Baum (Cambridge, Mass: Harvard University Press, 1928)

——, *The House of Life: A Sonnet-Sequence by Dante Gabriel Rossetti: A Variorum Edition*, ed. Roger C. Lewis (Woodbridge, Suffolk: Boydell & Brewer, 2007)

Scott, Walter, 'The Gathering Song of Donald Dhu' [1796], in *Poems Every Child Should Know*, ed. Mary Burt (New York: Grosset & Dunlap, 1904)

Sharp, William, ed., *Sonnets of This Century* (London: Walter Scott, 1888)

Spencer, Herbert, *Ecclesiastical Institutions: Principles of Sociology* (London: 1887)

Stanton, Elizabeth Cady, ed., *The Woman's Bible: the Passages in the Bible related to Women*, 2 vols (New York: European Publishing Company, 1895)

Strauss, David Friedrich, *The Life of Jesus Critically Examined*, trans. George Eliot (London: Chapman, 1846)

——, *The Old Faith and the New – A Confession*, 6th edn, trans. Mathilde Blind (London: Asher, 1873)

Swedenborg, Emanuel, *Angelic Wisdom concerning the Divine Providence* [1764] (London: The Swedenborg Society, 1857)

Tennyson, Alfred, *Poems of Alfred, Lord Tennyson, 1830–1858* (London: Grant Richards, 1903)

Tomson, Graham R. [Rosamund Marriott Watson], *Poets and Poetry of The Century: Robert Bridges and Contemporary Poets*, ed. Alfred H. Miles (London: Hutchinson, n.d. [1893])

'T.P.W.', 'The New Woman on the Bible', *Scottish Review* 30 (1897)

Tynan, Katharine, *Ballads and Lyrics* (London: Kegan Paul, Trench, 1891)

Waddington, Samuel, ed., *English Sonnets by Living Writers*, 2nd edn (London: George Bell and Sons, 1884)

Waring, Anna L., *Hymns and Meditations*, 2nd. edn (London: C. Gilpin, 1850)

Watson, Rosamund Marriott, *The Poems* (London: John Lane, 1912)

Webster, Augusta, *Portraits* (London: Macmillan and Co., 1870)

——, *Mother & Daughter, an Uncompleted Sonnet-sequence* (London: Macmillan and Co., 1895)

——, *Selections from the Verse of Augusta Webster* (London: Macmillan and Co., 1893)

Westminster Hymnal: The Only Collection Authorized by the Hierarchy of England and Wales (London: Burns Oates & Washbourne, 1912)

Williams, Isaac, *Cathedral, or the Catholic and Apostolic Church in England* (Oxford: John Henry Parker, 1838)

——, *The Baptistery, or, The Way of Eternal Life* (Oxford: J.H. Parker, 1842)

Wollstonecraft, Mary, *Vindication of the Rights of Women, with Strictures on Political and Moral Subjects* (London: St. Paul's Church Yard, 1792)

Yonge, Charlotte, ed., *The Child's Christian Year: Hymns for Every Sunday and Holy-Day*, 2nd edn (London: J. G. F. and J. Rivington, 1842)

SECONDARY SOURCES

Acland, Alice, *Caroline Norton* (London: Constable, 1948)

Adler, Alfred, 'Complex Compulsion as part of Personality and Neurosis', in *Superiority and Social Interest*, ed. L. and R. R. Ansbacher, rev. edn (New York: Viking, 1973)

Armstrong, Isobel, *Language as a Living Form in Nineteenth-Century Poetry* (Sussex: Harvester, 1982)

——, ed., *New Feminist Discourses: Critical Essays on Theories and Texts* (London: Routledge, 1992)

——, ed., *Victorian Poetry: Poetry, Poetics and Politics* (London: Routledge, 1993)

——, *Victorian Glassworlds: Glass Culture and the Imagination, 1830–1880* (Oxford: Oxford University Press, 2008)

——, Joseph Bristow, and Cath Sharrock, eds, *Nineteenth-Century Women Poets* (Oxford: Clarendon, 1996)

Armstrong, Karen, *A History of God from Abraham to the Present: the 4000-year Quest for God* (London: Heinemann: London, 1993)

——, *Gospel According to Woman* (London: Fount, 1996)

Ashe, Geoffrey, *From Caesar to Arthur* (London: Collins, 1960)

Ashton, Rosemary, ed., *Versatile Victorian: Selected Critical Writings of George Henry Lewes* (London: Bristol Classical Press, 1992)

Aune, Kristin, Sonya Sharma, and Giselle Vincett, eds, *Women and Religion in the West: Challenging Secularization* (Aldershot: Ashgate, 2008)

Beer, Gillian, *Darwin's Plots, Evolutionary Narrative in Darwin, George Eliot and Nineteenth-Century Fiction*, 2nd edn (Cambridge: Cambridge University Press, 2000)

Bewkes, Eugene Garrett, *Experience, Reason and Faith: A Survey in Philosophy and Religion* (London: Harper & Brothers Publishers, 1940)

Blain, Virginia, 'Women Poets and the Challenge of Genre', in *Women and Literature in Britain 1800–1900*, ed. Joanne Shattock (Cambridge: Cambridge University Press, 2001)

——, ed., *Victorian Women Poets: New Annotated Anthology*, rev edn (Longman, 2009)

Blair, Kirstie, ed., *John Keble in Context* (London: Anthem Press, 2007)

——, and Emma Mason, 'Tractarian Poets', *Victorian Poetry* 44 (2006)

Boos, Florence, 'Dante Gabriel Rossetti's Poetic Daughters: Fin-de-Siècle Women Poets and the Sonnet', in *Outsiders Looking In: The Rossettis Then and Now*, ed. David Clifford and Laurence Roussillon (London: Anthem Press, 2004)

Bown, Nicola, Carolyn Burdett and Pamela Thurschwell, eds, *The Victorian Supernatural* (Cambridge: Cambridge University Press, 2004)

Brennan, Catherine, Angers, *Fantasies and Ghostly Fears: Nineteen-Century Women from Wales & English-Language Poetry* (Cardiff: University of Wales, 2003)

Bristow, Joseph, ed., *The Victorian Poet: Poetics & Persona* (London: Croom Helm, 1987)

——, *The Cambridge Companion to Victorian Poetry* (Cambridge: Cambridge University Press, 2000)

Bronfen, Elisabeth, *Over Her Dead Body: Death, Femininity and the Aesthetic* (Manchester: Manchester University Press, 1992)

Brown, Daniel, 'Victorian Poetry and Science', in *Cambridge Companion to Victorian Poetry*, ed. Joseph Bristow (Cambridge: Cambridge University Press, 2000)

Bruzelius, Margaret, 'Mother's Pain, Mother's Voice: Gabriela Mistral, Julia Kristeva, and the Mater Dolorosa', *Tulsa Studies in Women's Literature* 18.2 (1999)

Buchanan, Robert ['Thomas Maitland'], 'Fleshly School of Poetry: Mr. D.G. Rossetti', *Contemporary Review* 18 (1871)

Burt, Mary, ed., *Poems Every Child Should Know*, (New York: Grosset & Dunlap, 1904)

Butler, J., *Gender Trouble: Feminism & the Subversion of Identity* (New York: Routledge, 1990)

Caine, T. Hall, ed., *Sonnets of Three Centuries: A Selection* (London: Elliot Stock, 1882)

Camp, Claudia V., 'Feminist Theological Hermeneutics: Canon and Christian Identity', in *Searching the Scriptures: A Feminist Introduction*, ed. Elisabeth Schüssler Fiorenza, 2 vols (London: SCM Press, 1994)

Campbell, Matthew, 'Poetry in the Four Nations' in *Companion to Victorian Poetry*, ed. Richard Cronin and others (Oxford: Blackwell, 2002)

Chadwick, Owen, *The Victorian Church*, 2nd edn, 2 vols, (London: Adam & Charles Black, 1970)

Chaucer, Geoffrey, *The Canterbury Tales*, ed. David Wright (Oxford: Oxford University Press, 1998)

Christ, Carol T., *Victorian and Modern Poetics* (London: The University of Chicago Press, 1984)

Church of Wales Committee, ed., *Morning and Evening Prayer, from the RSV of the Bible* (Oxford: Oxford University Press, 1961)

Clifford, Anne M., *Introducing Feminist Theology* (New York: Orbis, 2001)

Clifford, David, and Laurence Roussillon, eds, *Outsiders Looking In: The Rossettis Then and Now* (London: Anthem Press, 2004)

Collections Historical and Archaeological relating to Montgomeryshire and its Borders: Issued by the Powys Club for the Use of its Members 46 and 49 (1940)

Cowan, Edward J., ed., *Ballad in Scottish History* (East Linton: Tuckwell Press, 2000)

Cronin, Richard, *Colour and Experience in Nineteenth-Century Poetry* (Basingstoke: Macmillan Press, 1988)

Cunningham, Valentine, ed., *The Victorians: An Anthology of Poetry and Poetics* (Oxford: Blackwell, 2000)

Cupitt, Don, *The Sea of Faith* (London: British Broadcasting Company, 1984)

Daly, Mary, 'Spiritual Dimension of Women's Liberation', in *Reader in Feminist Knowledge*, ed. Sneja Gunew (London: Routledge, 1991)

D'Amico, Diane, *Christina Rossetti: Faith, Gender and Time* (Baton Rouge: Louisiana State University Press, 1999)

Dieleman, Karen, 'Elizabeth Barrett Browning's Religious Poetics: Congregationalist Models of Hymnist and Preacher', *Victorian Poetry*, 45 (2007)

Donne, John, *Poetical Works* [1633], ed. Herbert Grierson (London: Oxford University Press, 1933)

Drain, Susan, *The Anglican Church in Nineteenth-Century Britain: Hymns Ancient & Modern (1860–1875)* (Lampeter, Texts and Studies in Religion: The Edwin Mellen Press, 1989)

Du Maurier, Daphne, *The Infernal World of Branwell Brontë* (Harmondsworth: Penguin, 1960)

Faas, Ekbert, *Retreat into the Mind: Victorian Poetry and the Rise of Psychiatry* (Princeton: Princeton University Press, 1991)

Faber, Geoffrey, *Oxford Apostles: A Character Study of the Oxford Movement* (London: Faber & Faber, 1933)

Findlay, Arthur J., *Psychic Stream or Source and Growth of the Christian Faith* (London: Psychic Press Ltd., 1939)

Finke, Laurie A., and Martin B. Shichtman, *King Arthur and the Myth of History* (Gainsville, Florida: University Press of Florida, 2004)

Fox, Adam, *English Hymns and Hymn Writers* (London: Collins, 1947)

Freke, Timothy, and Peter Gandy, *The Jesus Mysteries* (London: Thorsons, 1999)

——, *Jesus and the Goddess: the Secret Teachings of the Original Christians* (London: Harper Collins, 2002)

Freud, Sigmund, *An Outline of Psychoanalysis*, trans. and ed. J. Strachey (New York: Norton, 1969)

Frye, Northrop, *Myth and Metaphor: Selected Essays 1974–1988*, ed. Robert D. Denham (London: University Press of Virginia, 1991)

Gill, Gregory, *The Life and Work of Adelaide Procter: Poetry, Feminism and Fathers* (Aldershot: Ashgate, 1998)

Gitter, Elisabeth G., 'The Power of Women's Hair in the Victorian Imagination', *PMLA* 99 (1984)

Goldenberg, Naomi R., *The Interpretation of the Flesh: Feminism, Psychoanalysis & the Resurrection of the Body* (Boston, USA: Beacon Press, 1990)

Goldin, Frederick, *The Mirror of Narcissus in the Courtly Love Lyric* (Ithaca: Cornell University Press, 1967)

Gospel According to Mary Magdalene, Gnostic Scripture and Fragments, Gnostic Society Library: <http://www.gnosis.org/library/marygosp.htm>

Gospel of Mary from the Nag Hammadi Library: <http://www.sol.com.au/kor/7_03.htm>

Gramish, Katie, and Catherine Brennan, eds, *Welsh Women's Poetry, 1460–2001* (Powys, Wales: Honno Classics, 2003)

Gray, F. Elizabeth, *The Christian and Lyric Tradition in Victorian Women's Poetry* (London: Routledge, 2010)

Guirand, Felix, ed., *Larousse Enclyclopedia of Mythology* (London: Batchworth Press, 1959)

Hall, Calvin S., *A Primer of Freudian Psychology* (New York: Mentor Books, 1959)

Haskins, Susan, *Mary Magdalen: Myth and Metaphor* (London: Harper Collins, 1993)

Hass, Andrew, David Jasper, and Elisabeth Jay, *The Oxford Handbook of English Literature and Theology* (Oxford: Oxford University Press, 2007)

Hassett, Constance W., *Christina Rossetti: the Patience of Style* (London: University of Virginia Press, 2005)

Hauke, Manfred, *Women in the Priesthood? A Systematic Analysis in the Light of the Order of Creation and Redemption*, trans. David Kipp (San Francisco: Ignatius Press, 1988)

Henwood, Dawn, 'Allegory and Subversive Poetics: Christina Rossetti's Prince's Progress Re-examined', *Victorian Poetry*, 35 (1996)

Hickok, Kathleen, 'Intimate Egoism': Reading and Evaluating Noncanonical Poetry by Women, *Victorian Poetry* 33 (1995)

——, 'Why is this Woman still Missing? Emily Pfeiffer, Victorian Poet', in *Women's Poetry, Late Romantic to Late Victorian: Gender and Genre, 1830–1900*, ed. Isobel Armstrong, and Virginia Blain (London: Palgrave Macmillan, 2002)

Hird, Myra J., 'Vacant Wombs: Feminist Challenges to Psychoanalytic Theories of Childless Women', *Feminist Review* 75 (2003)

Hoare, Philip, *England's Lost Eden: Adventures in a Victorian Utopia* (London: Fourth Estate, 2005)

Hogan, Anne, and Andrew Bradstock, eds, *Women of Faith in Victorian Culture: Reassessing the Angel in the House* (London: Macmillan Press Ltd., 1998)

Holmes, John Robert, *Dante Gabriel Rossetti and the Late Victorian Sonnet Sequence: Sexuality, Belief and the Self* (Aldershot: Ashgate, 2005)

Ingram, Penelope, 'From Goddess Spirituality to Irigaray's Angel: The Politics of the Divine', *Feminist Review* 66 (2000)

Jacobi, J., *The Psychology of Jung* (New Haven, USA: Yale University Press, 1962)

James, Frank, 'Science and Religion', *London Library Magazine* 12 (2011)

Jantzen, Grace M., Power, *Gender and Christian Mysticism* (Cambridge: Cambridge University Press, 1995)

Januszscak, Waldemar, 'Art Under Attack', *Sunday Times* (6 October 2013)

Jeffreys, Mark, 'Ideologies of Lyric: Problem of Genre in Contemporary Anglophone Poetics', *PMLA* 110 (1995)

Jenkins, Ruth Y., *Reclaiming Myths of Power, Women Writers and the Victorian Spiritual Crisis* (London: Associated University Presses, 1995)

Johnson, Elizabeth A., *She Who Is: The Mystery of God in Feminist Theological Discourse* (New York: The Crossroad Publishing Company, 1992)

Jung, Carl, *Psychological Types* (New York: Harcourt, 1923)

Keats, John, *Poems* (London: J. M. Dent, 1907)

Kern, Kathi, *Mrs. Stanton's Bible* (London: Cornell University Press, 2001)

Kerrigan, John, ed., *Motives of Woe: Shakespeare and 'Female Complaint'. A Critical Anthology* (Oxford: Clarendon Press, 1991)

King, Karen L., *Gospel of Mary of Magdala: Jesus and the First Woman Apostle* (Santa Rosa: Polebridge Press, 2003)

Knight, Mark, and Emma Mason, *Nineteenth-Century Religion and Literature: An Introduction* (Oxford: Oxford University Press, 2009)

Kohon, Gregorio, ed., *The British School of Psychoanalysis: The Independent Tradition* (London: Free Association Books, 1986)

Kristeva, Julia, 'Stabat Mater, the Paradox: Mother of Primary Narcissism', in *The Kristeva Reader*, ed. Toril Moi (Oxford: Blackwell, 1986)

Larsen, Timothy, *Crisis of Doubt: Honest Faith in Nineteenth-Century England* (Oxford University Press, 2006)

Legend of Lady's Rock: <http://www.clanlivingstone.com/ladyrock.htm>

Leighton, Angela, *Victorian Women Poets: Writing Against the Heart* (London: Harvester Wheatsheaf, 1992)

——, and Margaret Reynolds, eds, *Victorian Women Poets: Anthology* (Oxford: Blackwell, 1991)

Lennard, John, *Poetry Handbook: A Guide to Reading Poetry for Pleasure and Practical Criticism* (Oxford: Oxford University Press, 1996)

'Libra', *Womanhood and the Bible* (London: Theosophical Publishing Society, 1891)

Lootens, Tricia, *Lost Saints: Silence, Gender, and Victorian Literary Canonization* (London: University Press of Virginia, 1996)

Louis, Margot K., 'Gods and Mysteries: The Revival of Paganism and the Remaking of Mythography through the Nineteenth Century', *Victorian Studies* 47 (2005)

——, *Persephone Rises, 1860–1927: Mythography, Gender, and the Creation of a New Spirituality* (Farnham, Surrey: Ashgate, 2009)

Marx, Karl, and Frederick Engels, *On Britain*, 2nd edn (Moscow: Foreign Languages Publishing House, 1962)

Mason, Emma, '"Her Silence Speaks": Keble's Female Heirs', in *John Keble in Context*, ed. Kirstie Blair (London: Anthem Press, 2004)

——, *Women Poets of the Nineteenth Century* (Tavistock, Devon: Northcote House, 2006)

Matthews, Colin, *Nineteenth Century: The British Isles, 1815–1901* (Oxford: Oxford University Press, 2000)

Melnyk, Julie, '"Mighty Victims": Women Writers and the Feminization of Christ', *Victorian Literature and Culture* 31: 'Victorian Religion' (2003)

Milton, John, *Paradise Lost*, ed. Scott Elledge, 2nd edn (London: W. W. Norton & Co., 1993)

Mistral, Gabriela, 'La Mujer Fuerte', in *Desolacion* (New York: Instituto de las Españas, 1922)

Morgan, Sue, ed., *Women, Religion, and Feminism in Britain, 1750–1900* (Basingstoke: Palgrave Macmillan, 2002)

Morgan, Thaïs, 'Victorian Sage Discourse and the Feminine: An Introduction', in *Victorian Sages and Cultural Discourses: Renegotiating Gender and Power*, ed. Thaïs Morgan (New Brunswick: Rutgers University Press, 1990)

Morgan, Victoria, and Claire Williams, *Shaping Belief: Culture, Politics and Religion in Nineteenth-Century Writing* (Liverpool: Liverpool University Press, 2008)

Nennius, *British History and the Welsh Annals*, ed. and trans. John Morris (London: Phillimore and Co. Ltd., 1980)

Olverson, T. D., 'Worlds without Women: Emily Pfeiffer's Political Hellenism', in *Women Writers and the Dark Side of Late-Victorian Hellenism* (London: Palgrave Macmillan, 2010)

Oziek, Carolyn, 'The Feminist and the Bible: Hermeneutical Alternatives', in *Feminist Perspectives on Biblical Scholarship*, ed. A. Y. Collins (Chico, CA: Scholars Press, 1985)

Palazzo, Lynda, *Christina Rossetti's Feminist Theology* (London: Palgrave, 2002)

Phelan, Joseph, *The Nineteenth-Century Sonnet* (London: Palgrave Macmillan, 2005)

Plato, *The Republic of Plato*, trans. Francis Macdonald Cornford (London: Oxford University Press, 1941)

Poovey, Mary, '"Scenes of an Indelicate Nature": The Medical "Treatment" of Victorian Women', *Representations* 14 (1986)

Prins, Yopie, 'Victorian Meters', in *The Cambridge Companion to Victorian Poetry*, ed. Joseph Bristow (Cambridge: Cambridge University Press, 2000)

Raphael, Melissa, *Introducing Thealogy: Discourse on the Goddess* (Sheffield: Sheffield Academic Press, c. 1999)

Ruether, Rosemary Radford, 'The Future of Feminist Theology in the Academy', *Journal of the Academy of Religion* 53 (1985)

Ryckman, Richard, *Theories of Personality* (Pacific Grove, California: Brooks/Cole, 1989)

Scheinberg, Cynthia, 'Victorian Poetry and Religious Diversity', in *The Cambridge Companion to Victorian Poetry*, ed. Joseph Bristow (Cambridge: Cambridge University Press, 2000)

Schüssler Fiorenza, Elisabeth, ed., *Searching the Scriptures*, 2 vols (New York: Herder & Herder, 1994)

Shakespeare, William, *Sonnets and A Lover's Complaint*, ed. John Kerrigan (London: Penguin, 1986)

Shneidman, Edwin, *Voices of Death* (London: Bantam Books, 1982)

Showalter, Elaine, *A Literature of Their Own: British Women Novelists from Brontë to Lessing* (London: Virago, 1984)

Slinn, E. Warwick, 'Poetry', in *The Companion to Victorian Literature and Culture*, ed. Herbert F. Tucker (Oxford: Blackwell, 2002)

Tange, Andrea Kaston, 'Constance Naden and the Erotics of Evolution: Mating the Woman of Letters with the Man of Science', *Nineteenth-Century Literature* 61 (2006)

Tennyson, G. B., *Victorian Devotional Poetry: The Tractarian Mode* (London: Harvard University Press, 1981)

Thain, Marion, 'Scientific Wooing': Naden's Marriage of Science and Poetry', *Victorian Poetry* 41 (2003)

Vadillo, Ana Parejo, 'Immaterial Poetics: A. Mary F. Robinson and the Fin-de-Siècle Poem', *The Fin-de-Siècle Poem, English Literary Culture and the 1890s*, ed. Joseph Bristow (Athens, Ohio: Ohio University Press, 2005)

——, *Women Poets and Urban Aestheticism: Passengers of Modernity* (London: Palgrave Macmillan, 2005)

VanEsveld Adams, Kimberly, 'The Madonna and Anna Jameson', in *Woman's Theology in Great Britain: Transfiguring the Faith of Their Fathers*, ed. Julie Melnyk (London: Garland, 1998)

——, *Our Lady of Victorian Feminism, The Madonna in the Work of Anna Jameson, Margaret Fuller and George Eliot* (Athens: Ohio University Press, 2001)

Vincett, Giselle, ed., *Women and Religion in the West: Challenging Secularization* (Aldershot: Ashgate, 2008)

Wade, J.H. and G.W., *History of Monmouthshire* (London: Methuen, 1909)

Walley, Noel, 'The Saints of North Wales: Saint Melangell': <www.greatorme.org.uk/melangell.html>

Warner, Marina, *Alone of All Her Sex: The Myth and Cult of the Virgin Mary* (London: Vintage, 1976)

Watson, J. R., 'Ancient or Modern, *Ancient and Modern*: The Victorian Hymn and the Nineteenth Century', *Yearbook of English Studies* 36 (2006)

Weston, Jessie L., *From Ritual to Romance* (Cambridge: Cambridge University Press, 1920)

Wheeler, Michael, *Heaven, Hell and the Victorians* (Cambridge: Cambridge University Press, 2001)

Willburn, Sarah A., *Possessed Victorians: Extra Spheres in Nineteenth-Century Mystical Writings* (Aldershot: Ashgate, 2006)

Wilson, A. N., *God's Funeral* (London: John Murray, 1999)

Woolf, Virginia, *A Room of One's Own* (London: Penguin Books, 1993)

INDEX

Adams, Kimberly VanEsveld 56, 59
Adler, Alfred 127
Alexander, Cecil Frances 24
Armstrong, Isobel 19–21
Arnold, Matthew 113–14
Aune, Kristin 14

Bachofen, Johann Jakob 17
Baillie, Joanna 111
Barrett Browning, Elizabeth 2–3, 14, 28–9, 42–3, 67; *Aurora Leigh* 2–3,
    29–30, 43, 67, 122–3, 126–7; 'Human Life's Mystery' 28; 'Lessons
    from the Gorse' 53, 80 (*n*.1); *Sonnets from the Portuguese* 42–4, 67
Beer, Gillian 45–6
Bevington, Louisa 6
Bewkes, Eugene 129
Blackie, John Stuart 2
Blind, Mathilde 6, 67, 115
Boismont, Brierre de 75
Book of Common Prayer, The 11, 23
Brennan, Catherine 86
Bronfen, Elisabeth 41–2, 130
Brontë, Ann 21–2
Brontë, Emily 21–2
Browning, Robert 128, 131–4
Bruzelius, Margaret 64
Burns, Robert 114
Butler, Josephine 116
Byron, George Gordon, Lord 4

Caine, Thomas Hall 46–7
Camp, Claudia 115
Campbell, Matthew 113
Carlyle, Thomas 9–10, 23, 30
Chaucer, Geoffrey 105–6, 114
Churchill, Winston 85–7
Clarke, Lowther 23
Cobbe, Frances Power 3, 95
Colenso, Bishop John 115

Coleridge, Samuel Taylor 131–2, 136–7
Constantine I 10
Cronin, Richard 132, 138

Damer, Anne Seymour 111
D'Amico, Diane 33, 67
Dante 10
Darwin, Charles 3, 12, 41, 45–6
Davis, Caroline 6 (*n.*1)
Davis, Thomas Richard 1–2, 86
Dickens, Charles 106
Dieleman, Karen 29–30
Draper, John William 45

Eliot, George (Marian Evans) 115

Faithful, Emily 2
Faraday, Michael 45
Field, Michael (Katharine Harris Bradley) 6, 42
Findlay, Arthur 95
Finke, Laurie 84–7
Fiorenza, Elisabeth Schüssler 12, 114–15
Freud, Sigmund 75
Froebel, Friedrich 51 (*n.*44)

Gatty, Margaret 46
Gray, Elizabeth 16
Greenough, Sarah Dana 67
Greenwell, Dora 14, 22, 24–5, 40, 67

Harrison, Jane Ellen 10–11, 61, 115, 129–30, 146
Havergal, Frances 24, 40
Hemans, Felicia 14, 20, 33
Herbert, George 51 (*n.*50)
Hickey, Emily 6
Hinkson, Katharine Tynan 6, 49 (*n.*5)
Hughes, Elizabeth 6

James, Frank 45
Jameson, Anna 56–7
Januszczak, Waldemar 59
Keats, John 113, 123, 131–2

Keble, John 23–6
Kingsley, Charles 45–6
Knight, Mark 44–5
Kristeva, Julia 58

Landon, Letitia 14, 20
Leakey, Caroline 24
Levy, Amy 67
Lewes, G. H. 45
Lootens, Tricia 42–3
Louis, Margot K. 13, 68–9, 88–9, 101
Lowie, Robert H. 129

Macpherson, James 113
Mason, Emma 23–4, 44–5
Melnyk, Julie 116
Meredith, George 51 (*n.*62)
Meynell, Alice 49 (*n.*5)
Mill, John Stuart 2, 55, 120
Milton, John 4
Mistral, Gabriela 64
Morgan, Thaïs 29, 36
Morris, William 113, 123

Naden, Constance 49 (*n.*10)
Newman, John 23
Nightingale, Florence 116
Norton, Caroline 2

Olverson, T. D. 2–3, 42
Osiek, Carolyn 115–16

Page, H. A. 24–6, 40
Parkes, Bessie Rayner [Belloc] 2, 24
Pattison, Mark 2
Pfeiffer (née Davis), Emily
LIFE 1–7, 34
WORKS 'Chrysalis, The' 4, 46–8; 'Coming Day, The' 48–9; 'Crown of Song, The' 4, 15, 28–34, 111; 'Everild' 14, 20–2; 'Fallen from Grace' 41; *Flowers of the Night* 6, 48; *Flying Leaves from East and West* 5–6, 102 (*n.*15); 'From Out of the Night' 15, 53, 66–80; 'Gerard's Monument' 14–15, 19–20; *Gerard's Monument, and Other*

Poems 3, 5, 19–20; *Glân-Alarch, His Silence and Song* 5, 15–16, 80, 83–102, 111, 123; 'He that is washed needs but to wash his feet' 26–8; 'Hellas' 7; *Holly-Branch, The* 1–2; 'Hymn to the Dark Christmas of 1874' 4, 15, 33–40; 'Madonna Dunya' 5, 15, 53, 55–66, 79–80, 111; *Margaret; or, The Motherless* 2–3; 'Outlawed' 2; *Poems* 4–5; *Quarterman's Grace and Other Poems* 5; *Rhyme of the Lady of the Rock, and How It Grew, The* 5, 9, 16, 102, 105–42; 'Song of Winter, A' 15, 53–5, 79; *Sonnets* 5; *Sonnets and Songs* 5, 40–1; 'Studies from the Antique' 2; *Under the Aspens, Lyrical and Dramatic* 5; 'Under the Rose' 41–2; *Valisneria, or A Midsummer Day's Dream* 2, 22, 30; *Women and Work* 3
Pfeiffer, Jürgen Edward 2–3, 86, 110
Phelan, Joseph 42–4
Plato 5
Pohle, Joseph 57–8
Preuss, Arthur 57–8
Procter, Adelaide Anne 22, 24, 53, 67
Pusey, Edward 23, 115

Rebus, Arthur 129
Renan, Ernest 115
Reynolds, Margaret 74
Richardson, Mary 59
Robinson, A. Mary F. 6
Rossetti, Christina 33, 42–4; 'Goblin Market' 67; *Monna Innominata* 43–4; 'My Dream' 53, 132; 'Paradise' 33
Rossetti, Dante Gabriel 43–4, 113
Rossetti, William 20
Ruether, Rosemary Radford 12

Scott, Walter 113, 132
Shakespeare, William 4, 10
Shichtman, Martin 84–7
Slinn, Warwick 42
Smith, Barabara Leigh [Bodichon] 2
Sophocles 102 (*n.*15)
Stanton, Elizabeth Cady 12–13, 56, 112
Stekel, Wilhelm 75
Strauss, David Friedrich 115
Swanwick, Anna 3
Swedenborg, Emanuel 49 (*n.*10)
Swinburne, Algernon 69

Taylor, Harriet 2, 55, 120
Tennyson, Alfred, Lord 113, 123, 131
Tennyson, G. B. 24, 28, 44
Tilsley, Emily 1, 86
Tilsey, William 7 (*n.*3)
Tyndall, John 45

Vadillo, Ana Parejo 6
Vincett, Giselle 14

Waring, Anna Letitia 14, 25–6, 28, 40
Warner, Marina 58–9
Watson, Rosamund Marriott (Tomson) 6, 49 (*n.*5)
Watts, Theodore 46
Webster, Augusta 6, 67
Wilson, A. N. 45
Wordsworth, William 4